EDDIE'S METHOD

Michael Walsh

America Star Books

Hardluxe 9781682292259
Hardback 9781451278354
Softcover 9781451278347
eBook 9781682295915
PUBLISHED BY AMERICA STAR BOOKS, LLLP
www.AmericaStarBooks.pub

This book is dedicated to the memory of my older brother
John who lived his life "Hanging in there with Jesus."
And to our mother who has always believed in me.

ACKNOWLEDGEMENT

Whenever someone writes a story similar to this one they quickly understand that they cannot do it alone. No matter what you write, or how you write it, inputs are required to fulfill the document.

Like everyone else I did have assistance in these areas. Certain people contributed greatly to the content and structure of this document. The first of which was my brother, Joe Walsh, who was instrumental in contributing structure and content to the story. His wife, Bonnie Walsh, assisted me in putting my emotions on paper. And that was not an easy task for her. Another contributor was their daughter, Rhea Walsh, who assisted me in the structure and editing. (Something I needed.) My neighbor and friend, Robert Fuller, also contributed by editing the document and consistently encouraging me not to give up during this process.

After reading this document I realized a few things. First of all, the content of this story is focused on just one portion of a large organization. This portion of that organization that this story is written about is the one that I was close to. Because of that it is the only part of the organization that I am comfortable writing about. There were hundreds of people who have taken part in the overall organization through the years and I do what to apologize for not mentioning any of them throughout this story. It was not intentional. In fact I would like to let each and everyone of them know that I am proud of every moment that I spent with them during this activity.

Throughout my experience with this organization one thing was constant. Two men, Eddie Fournier and Bill Smith, were always there to help us. You see they were our friends, our confidants, and our mentors. And to many of us they are **great** men. They impacted our lives greatly. And many of us could not get through the incidents mentioned in this book with out their assistance.

PART ONE

Spring

It was the spring of 1961. I was walking down Sackett Street in Westfield, Massachusetts. The snow from the winter was gone now and the air was once again clear from the change in the season and the flowers were beginning to bloom. The fragrance of spring was everywhere. The scent was relaxing and invigorating at the same time.

Our neighborhood was about a half a mile away from the activities of Main Street keeping us isolated from the hustle and bustle of downtown. The street was a mixture of cultures. At the end there were Polish families, in the middle were Italian families, and most recently a Puerto Rican family had moved in across the street from us.

It was a narrow street; it measured about two car widths across. Fortunately, there was very little traffic and no one parked on the street itself because if they had it would have been difficult for anyone to get around them.

I was a very self-conscious thirteen-year-old, always looking around checking out everything around me. I stood about 5 feet 6 inches tall and weighed approximately 150 pounds. I didn't think I was over weight but anyone who saw me would definitely disagree. I was a very typical thirteen-year-old boy with short brown hair and no concept of reality.

As I came around the corner of the street I could see my house. I was now walking next to my grandmother's house. It was a narrow two-story house with green shutters set on the corner of the lot that was a quarter of an acre. The house was divided into two apartments. My grandmother, who was my father's mother, lived on the first floor and rented out the other apartment upstairs from her.

Her front porch was on Orange Street while the back porch faced our street. As I came even to her back of her house I could see the screened in porch that she used as an entrance. And the only thought that came to mind was I do not want to see her today. At the end of her yard was a wire fence about four feet high with a rusted metal pole stuck in the ground to tie it off. On the other side of this fence was the sidewalk leading to our house. Ours was a green two-story house with a covered front porch that was set back about a hundred feet from the street. I could still remember how difficult it was to shovel that long sidewalk during the winter. My older brother and I always got to do this little chore and it was a tough one that I despised doing.

Then something caught my attention from the corner of my eye. It was smoke, and it looked like it was coming from the house across the street from ours.

The house was painted gray with a white porch in the front and the back. It was subdivided into two apartments. I walked a little quicker now; I wanted to know what it was that I saw.

As I got close to the front of the house there was no sign of any smoke from there. I continued walking. I couldn't see anything from the side either. Then, as I got to the back of the house, there it was. Smoke was pouring out of the clapboards of the house. The gray paint on the outside of the house was covered in a blanket of smoke.

Suddenly I heard a voice behind me. It was a man in his thirties, on his way home from working at the water department that was located at the end of the street. His jacket had the emblem of our local water department on it. He stood about six feet tall, wore a light blue jacket, and had salt and pepper hair. His voice was deep and loud. And when he spoke I felt nothing but panic. I froze at first. I didn't know how to respond.

The man spoke again, this time in a yell, "Do you live around here? Call the fire department now."

I didn't know what else to do so I took off across the street to our house to call the fire department. The panic in his voice had motivated me to do something. I couldn't say anything. I just ran home to call the fire department. His tone had instilled panic in me and I just wanted to end that feeling as quickly as I could.

When I got to the house my mother and my three brothers were all home. I came in yelling to my mother, "Call the fire department quick, the house across the street is on fire".

My mother just looked at me in amazement. My older brother went to the phone and started dialing. He asked me, "Which house?"

I told him the one across the street. Once my brother got off the phone you could hear the sirens off in a distance. Fortunately, the fire department was located less than a mile from where we lived.

It was now that I decided to go see what was going on. My mother told me to stay home. But I wasn't having anything to do with that. In her own way she wanted to protect me and

I knew it. She just didn't want me to take any chances but I needed to know what had happened. So I went back across the street to find out.

By the time I got back to the burning house the firemen were showing up. They set up very quickly.

The man from the water department was still there standing out in front of the house. I joined him. We were both standing there when the Fire Chief came over to talk to us. He asked: " Do either one of you live here?"

We told him no, that we were both just walking by when we noticed the fire.

His response was, "Thanks for calling. Now please step back out of the way so we can do our job".

It was then that a woman came running up to the house. She was yelling in broken English, "My babies, my babies where are they? You have to go get my babies".

My heart dropped. It felt like someone had just pulled the world out from under me. I could see complete anguish on the face of the man from the water department. And I understood why.

The Fire Chief ran to her. He kept repeating, "Where are they? Where are they? How old are they?"

You could see that she understood what he was asking and she was trying to contain herself enough to explain that they were in a bedroom upstairs in the back of the house.

As soon as he understood what she was saying. He called two of the firemen over and told them that there were two six-month old infants inside. It took almost no time for the two firemen to get outfitted with air tanks and masks. When they broke into the front door with their axes a wall of smoke came pouring out. And in they went.

The man from the water department, and I just stood there waiting for some sign of the two firemen and the children. The wait was painful we could both feel the anxiety of the moment. It seemed like it was taking forever. Each second felt like an eternity. All we could do was stand and wait. They were not coming out. I just wondered if they found the infants yet. The house was not that big. Why is it taking so long? Why haven't they brought the children out yet?

Suddenly, the two firemen came out each holding a young infant in their arms. They both had a look of concern in their eyes. As they got out of the house they threw off their masks and started performing CPR on the infants.

The man from the water department looked at me and said, "That's not a good sign".

All I could do was stare at the firemen performing CPR on the infants. They just kept working on the children.

After about three minutes they stopped trying to revive the children. Both firemen had a very strained look on their faces. They went over to the mother. They spoke to her, and she broke into hysterical tears and fell to the ground. Neither the man from the water department nor I knew what was going on we just looked at each other with questioning looks. We had no idea what all this meant.

The Fire Chief came over to us. Slowly, he explained that we both deserved to know what just happened. He said, " We were too late, we tried to save them but they are dead from smoke inhalation."

Before either myself, or the man from the water department could say anything he also added, "And just to let you guys know, if you had tried to rescue them the smoke would have killed you too. Without breathing equipment no one was going to live going into that house."

That last statement didn't mean much to me. And from what I could see it didn't mean much to the man from the water department either. We were both in tears at this point. I had never seen anyone die before. And to have it be two infants I just couldn't believe it. I was in shock. I was feeling a mixture of emotions, what if I had gone in the burning house before calling the fire department, could the babies still be alive?

This was the nagging question. I didn't like this heartache or emptiness that I now felt. There was a pain that I could not explain and it wasn't going away. I just continued to cry. The Fire Chief then put his arm around me and asked, "Where do you live son? "

I could only lift my arm and point in the direction of my house. The chief then called over one of the other firemen and asked him to bring me home and explain what happened.

When we got to my house, my mother was in panic. She didn't know what to say or do. She only hugged me. I was still crying when I went upstairs to my room. My younger brothers tried to find out what happened but I was not talking. I just couldn't share what I had just seen with anyone.

My father came home a little later. He was a thin man with gray hair and a muscular frame. He had been in the Navy during World War II and had seen some action in the Pacific. After my mother explained what had happened to me he came upstairs to talk to me. I was not ready to talk to anyone. I was just completely depressed by what I had just seen. It was tearing me apart. I didn't know how to deal with it. And at that moment I realized that I would never forget what had just happened.

My father was a strong man who never let out his emotions. This day was going to be different. He struggled trying to talk to me at first, then started to relate what it felt like loosing good friends during the war. Friends he would never see again. Both he and I cried together. He also told me that it was okay to cry. It was time to let it out. All this was helpful to me at the time but the damage was done and there was darkness in my heart that I could not explain. All I knew was that I really didn't care about much anymore. And as far as I was concerned that feeling was going to be with me forever. After all two infants had just died right in front of me. And the emptiness left within me from that experience was devastating. I suddenly had no feelings at all. I was empty. I felt like nothing could ever touch me emotionally again.

So the only thing that I could do was drive these emotions deep inside myself, so deep that I couldn't feel them anymore. I could feel anger swelling inside of me, anger like no other I had felt before. And this one was not going away. And as long as I had it no one could hurt me anymore. After all I already felt the worst pain I could possibly imagine. And the worst part was that I was still around to experience it.

Summer

Before this incident I was already on my way to being a very bitter young man. It had all started a couple of years earlier when I realized that I was the invisible member of my family to our relatives.

Our grandmother, my father's mother, had started it. She would shower my older brother with gifts and trips constantly while I sat at home wondering when it was going to be my turn. And then I found out from her that she only had one grandson and it was my brother and not I. She had done this while visiting us. And what is even worse she did it after I had mustered the courage to ask her when I was going to go on a trip with her. That revelation bothered me a lot. I felt like she was leaving me out intentionally. I was hurt by it. And I didn't like that feeling at all. It was clear to her that I didn't exist and I didn't like being ignored even by her.

But when my mother's family starting showering my younger brothers with gifts and trips it really bothered me. I really felt left out now and I was getting angry about it. It was not a good feeling to have your relatives give gifts to your older brother and your younger brothers and not even acknowledge your existence in the process. I was angry all the time over being ignored by them. And I didn't care if they didn't like it. In fact I didn't care how they felt about.

John, my older brother, would often come to me afterwards and tell me how bad he felt about it. I know he was trying to help, but it just made matters worse for me. I didn't need him feeling sorry for me. There was no need for any pity comments from him as far as I was concerned.

I did have one bright spot though. My mother did have one brother who treated me as if I was a human being. It was her brother, my Uncle Roger and his wife, my Aunt Rose. Whenever they came to visit they treated me like an equal. And it felt good to have someone respect me. They were always interested in what I thought. And he was constantly interested in how I felt about everything. He even told me that he firmly believed that I was going to do something really *great* some day. That was a complete surprise to me. Someone thought I was worth something. I didn't completely understand what he meant by that but it felt good to have someone say that they had confidence in me. That vote of confidence was the one thing I looked forward to in their visits. I was always happy when they were around. I would look forward to their visits for weeks. Unfortunately we only got to see them once or twice a year. And that bothered me a lot. They lived in Connecticut and had four young children of their own to deal with at that time. Consequently they could only visit on rare occasions. In between visits I was getting more and more defiant all the time. And the more I thought about how the other relatives treated me the more defiant I became.

The person that I was getting the most defiant with was my mother. I would push and push her until she responded to me in anger. I didn't feel good about doing this, it hurt me to do this, but her emotional outburst were reassurance that I was noticed. And at this point negative reinforcement to me was better than none at all.

If you couple these feelings along with the ones from the death of the two six-month old infants you can understand why I was becoming a very bitter, angry, and defiant young man.

During this time my family was trying to help me through my emotional issues in their own way with no success. My mother would tell me that, "You just have to get over it: there is nothing you could do about it".

You see my mother had grownup during the great depression. She had learned to deal with very difficult things anyway she could. She had always found a way to release her emotions during that period. She was trying to help me find a way to release my emotions and get on with my life. It wasn't working. I hadn't found anything that would get rid of them. And as far as I was concerned I never would.

My father was constantly trying to talk to me about it but I did not want anything to do with that conversation. In my mind I had driven the emotions deep inside of myself and the last thing I wanted to do was bring them back up through discussion. I had turned very cold toward everything. I was feeling nothing. For the first time in my life I had all of my emotions in complete check, and I liked my safe little world. Besides what did it matter, I was invisible to just about all of the people we called relatives. I didn't exist in their minds. And as long as I had no feelings it didn't matter to me at all.

My older brother John took a different approach. He would say, "If the death of those two babies bothered you that much why didn't you do something to save them"?

You know that was *not* the question I wanted to hear. The only thing John's question managed to do was to make me angry and I wanted to get even with my brother for bringing it back up.

At first I couldn't quite figure out how to get John to stop asking that question. But I found a way. I realized that my brother had a very explosive temper and I was the one person who knew how to trigger it. You see John was about an inch shorter than me at this time, and I knew how to use it against him. So whenever John would start asking me that question I would respond with, "Don't worry about it little brother".

This always sparked a response in John. He would respond by saying: "I am your older brother and *not your little brother*." And then he would start attacking me physically in an effort to prove his point. What you have to know is that John was two years older than me, twice my size in bulk, and about three times stronger than I was.

But I had an advantage. I was faster than John. And whenever we would have one of these confrontations I would take off running into the neighborhood. John would always stop chasing me about a hundred yards down the street and yell, "Just remember I know where you live".

I would just laugh and say " And by the time I come home you will have calmed down, or I will just stick near Mom so you can't touch me".

She would always protect me whenever John had lost his temper. I knew that no matter what I tried there was no controlling my older brother once he lost his temper. And I had learned, the hard way, that you didn't want to be on the receiving side of John's anger. The only person who ever had success in calming John down was our mother. And I was going to use that fact whenever I had to.

On one of these occasions, when I was running from John, I was met by an acquaintance of mine called Doug.

He just stood in front of his house laughing and said, "You know one of these days he is going to catch you and I don't want to be around when he does".

I just laughed and said "Your not alone in that one."

From that point on Doug and I started becoming friends. He stood about a half inch shorter than me with a stocky build and an attitude of someone who just loved life. He was full of one-liners that would constantly make me laugh. One of his favorite saying was that "I eat to live and live to eat". If you happened to ask him what he was doing he would respond with " Posing for animal crackers". These one-liners helped me to forget and begin to feel normal again. They were an emotional release for me and I needed it. I quickly understood something about him that very few people ever would. It was that the more obnoxious the comments he made simply meant that he was impressed about whatever he was commenting on. So the goal for me was to get as many really obnoxious comments out of him as I could. It was a little game we both played and I enjoyed it. I would do or say something and he would respond with a really obnoxious comment. This in turn would get a quick response from everyone around us. We were having fun with this little game of ours. No one else understood it. But we did and that was all that mattered.

He and I started sharing our lives. We both had older brothers that frustrated us. And we both were bitter about our lives to that point. You see Doug was also invisible to his relatives. Doug had two older brothers who had both done well in school as well as in high school athletics. All of Doug's relative's were constantly showering praises and accolades on them because of it. And that made him feel like he was completely left out of everything just like I did.

I, on the other hand, had my brother John, who I had tried to compete with constantly and couldn't succeed with it no matter what I did. My father's relatives still felt that he was the only member of our family. This feeling of being invisible was very frustrating for both Doug and myself. We had no idea how to respond to it. So we responded in the only way we could. We rebelled whenever we had the chance.

Fortunately, for me, my brother John had joined a drum corps during the spring. Now this did not bother me in the least. You see John played the trumpet in the high school band. And he was playing this same trumpet in the drum corps. For years all I had heard was John playing the scales on his trumpet. And I used to ask him, "Don't you know anything else?"

John would just laugh and say that he was going to continue practicing that until he couldn't get it wrong. I was dumbfounded by his response. After all to me that concept didn't make any sense. And every time I would go outside of the yard when John was practicing, all of the neighbors would ask me the same question, "Doesn't he know another song"?

I would just laugh and say, "I guess not".

At the end of the street where we lived there was a small dyke by the Westfield River. It was about forty feet high. It was all grown over with vegetation now but I could remember how it had held back a flood about five years earlier.

I remember my father bringing John and myself to the top of the dyke to show us the water level at that time. When we got to the top I was amazed. The river had swollen to about a half a mile wide, when it was normally twenty- yards in width, and was just five feet from coming over the dyke and into our street.

Our father did tell us that the water level was receding and we had nothing to be afraid of. All I could think of was that I had no idea that we were that close to being flooded out of our home that year. Because if that much water did come over the dyke I am certain that is would have taken our house with it.

This area of dense vegetation, where the floodwaters once were, is where Doug and I hung around. We had befriended two other teenagers there. The two were older than Doug and I, both were two years older than Doug and that put them three years my senior, but they wanted us two younger guys to hang around with them. We were impressed. Some older guys wanted to be with us. They accepted us as their equal. To them we were not invisible. And that fact was important to us both.

Danny was about six feet tall and had a muscular frame while Larry was about two inches shorter than me and he was built like a body builder.

They started off just talking to Doug and me, and gradually they introduced us to smoking and drinking beer. Now this was fun for us. We got to act like adults without anyone looking over their shoulder and judging us. It was another emotional release for me and I was enjoying it. It gave me a chance to express myself in a way that I had never done before. And as long as Doug was there with me I felt completely comfortable. It didn't matter what we did or how we did it as far as I was concerned. We were both enjoying the fact we were considered equals by these two. And that meant a lot to both of us.

Larry and Danny kept talking about how they would all look out for each other and protect each other when it was needed. That was okay with us, especially since we had thought we had found someone who finally understood us.

And besides I couldn't imagine any situation coming up that we would need protection from. And until that situation comes up I was going to enjoy myself as much as I could. After all this was the group of people that I could be with that didn't mind if I got a little rebellious. In fact they encouraged it.

One day Larry asked us if we had any money for beer and smokes. Neither one of us had any cash. So Larry just told us to come with him: they would go get some. We followed him to the top of the dyke and Larry just stopped. Doug asked him, "Where are we going? "

Larry responded with, " Just wait here and you'll see".

It turns out that there were a lot of alcoholics in our little town that would go to the liquor store after getting paid, drink whatever they had purchased and walk down to the dyke to find a place to sleep it off, before they went home for the day. This was the first time that I had noticed it. In fact this was the first time I was even aware of these activities. We just stood there watching a couple of them as they went through their process. It was very disturbing watching someone who had no control of their facilities trying to settle down for a nap before they went home to their families. Once they fell asleep Danny proceeded to tell us the plan.

It was simple enough. They would wait until an alcoholic was passed out and go over and pick his pockets for whatever cash he had left on him. He then explained that they would never know the difference. They would just believe that they had spent it when they woke up. According to Danny whenever these individuals starting drinking they didn't care about anything but drinking. And as far as they were concerned if the money was gone, that meant that they spent it on getting drunk.

The idea of taking advantage of someone while they were sleeping, drunk or not, bothered me. To me it was stealing no matter which way you justified it. But I knew that if I wanted to continue being with these two we had to take part in some of these activities. Immediately I rationalized everything to myself by saying that if I didn't actually do the stealing I could not be held responsible for it. And in that way I could accept taking part in some of these activities.

The first couple of times they did this Doug and I just watched. It did bother me to see them stealing the money. But I kept rationalizing it. I just kept saying to myself as long as I am not doing the stealing I am not responsible. This worked for the next couple of weeks. During this time it was not unusual for us to take twenty to forty dollars from these individuals while they were passed out. It was usually enough to keep us all in beer and cigarettes for at least a week at a time. Eventually, Larry and Danny wanted us to get involved in getting the money. That day had finally arrived. The person involved was younger and better dressed than the others we had seen and he was taking a long time to pass out. When it seemed like he did, Larry said, " Go get it".

About now I was having a real conflict going on inside of me. I was regretting my decision to ever take part in this activity. I knew it was wrong. I knew it was stealing. But I also knew that if we didn't do it we would be in big trouble with the other two. And that thought bothered me quite a bit. I was scared. I felt like I was being forced to do something very wrong, And yet I didn't feel like I had any other choice in the matter.

So Doug and I went over to him and started to pick through his pockets.

He stirred and said, " What are you doing, that money is for my kids. What are you doing"?

We could hear Larry in the background behind them saying, "Hit him."

I just stood there in a panic. He wanted someone to do what? I didn't agree to beat anyone up for this. I could only stand there in panic. That would be wrong in my mind. To take advantage of someone passed out was bad enough in my mind. But to physically hurt him was an issue that I didn't want any part of.

Then from nowhere came Danny with a large stick. He hit the man. The man slumped down. Now I was really scared. He didn't move. I wasn't sure if he was still breathing or not. I asked Doug, " Is he okay".

Doug looked at him and turned to me and said, " Yea, he is only knocked out".

We didn't know what to do at first. I started panicking. Doug just turned to me and said: " Let's get out of here."

I could only nod in response.

All four of us ran off quickly. We took off in two different directions.

Doug and I were running together through the vegetation when I said to him, " I don't like what we just did."

He just looked at me and said," I agree with you."

I could only say," I don't care how we do it. But somehow we have to get out of doing this again."

He just looked at me while we were running and said," I agree with you. I just don't know how we are going to do it."

What we had just seen bothered both of us. We both felt remorse and guilt over what had just happened. It was a feeling that neither one of us ever wanted to have again.

We had previously designated a location in the brush where we would always meet if something happened. And this was one of those times. Our meeting place was about a half a mile away. It was a position about fifty yards from the Westfield River, on a large round rock. When we got there Larry asked for the money so he could see how much there was. Doug gave it to him. He looked at me and we both seemed to feel the same about what had just happened. It was like he was trying to tell me something. I could tell that things had gone too far for him. And I was feeling the same way. We didn't like what we just saw, and we didn't want to have any part of this activity from then on. The guilt was just too much for either one of us to handle. And I could tell from his look that it was now or never for us to get out of this situation.

Doug turned and said to Larry, "Keep it, I don't want any part of it" and started to walk away.

I started to walk away also saying, "I'm with him".

Larry was losing his mind; he kept yelling, "You can't leave now. If you do I will beat the shit out of you every time I see you on the street, and remember, Doug I know where you live".

Doug and I just kept walking. We didn't dare turn around. After all we had a pretty good idea what these two were capable of, and we did not want to have anything to do with it. Especially since we now had a better idea of just how ruthless these two could be. I could feel my heart beating loudly as we walked away. I was scared and I knew it. We both knew that it was the right thing to do. We had to get out of there as quickly as we could. And yet we were both concerned about what Larry might do if he caught up to us.

We just whispered back and forth. I said to Doug, "He does know where you live".

Doug's response was, "Yea, but he doesn't know where your house is, so guess where we are going".

My response was simple, "Who knows, maybe this is one of the times that my older brother might come in handy for a change". And we both smiled to each other. After all John's temper was well known throughout the neighborhood. And this could be one situation where it might be useful to us both. Not that I thought John would protect us. Instead I knew that if he had ever found out what we had taken part in he would proceed to beat us both up. I was just hoping that his presence might be enough to give Larry second thoughts if it ever came down to it.

From that day on Doug was always at my house. He stayed at his house long enough to sleep and get dressed, and then he was off to see if I was awake yet.

26

Because of Larry's threat I was happy that my father had signed me up for Babe Ruth baseball in the spring. To my surprise a team had picked me. And I now had something to do that would keep me away from contact with Larry, at least temporarily. I had played little league baseball in the local league. So I did have some experience in this area.

I was left-handed and could hit a baseball to right center and right field whenever I wanted to. Unfortunately, my catching ability and my throwing arm were very suspect. So much so in fact that my new coach had told me that I had to do some work in order to improve those skills. That information didn't bother me in the least. I knew I needed work in those areas. All I was looking for was someone to teach me. And from the looks of things he might have been the right person. After all he did correctly identify my playing weaknesses very quickly.

Whenever I would go to practices or games Doug would go with me. After all Doug and I were both in this thing together. We were both trying to stay out of the neighborhood and out of contact with Larry and his threat. It turns out that I could still hit a baseball. And that was a pleasant surprise to me. During the season I was up to bat five times. The results were disappointing. If I didn't strike out, I hit the ball directly to the first baseman. I was discouraged. This was not what I had envisioned at all. This is something that I wanted to do, and it wasn't working out. I was depressed about my whole baseball experience. As much as I wanted this to work out, it just wouldn't. It was just typical for me. I was once again the invisible one. And I wasn't very happy with myself because of it. Because this time it was me that caused it and no one else had anything to do with it. I was considering quitting at the end of the season. After all that is what I typically did whenever things didn't work out for me.

I had been in the Boy Scouts and couldn't get myself to be productive in attaining merit badges, so I just quit. I had been an alter boy at our church and finally just quit when I got tired of the discipline. This was my pattern. Whenever something got difficult for me I would just quit doing it. And it looked like baseball was going to be another one of these activities in that pattern.

As the season came to a close, the team I was on ended up in the playoffs. What this meant was that each team played in a single elimination tournament and if we lost a game we were eliminated from that tournament. Somehow my team made it all the way to the final game. I didn't play in any of the games for them to get there. And in my mind that was a good thing. Namely, because I felt that if I had played in any of the games we wouldn't have made it to the Championship game.

As the final game progressed it became clear that this was going to be a hard fought battle. The opposing team was the first to score two runs in the fourth inning. My team scored two runs in the eighth inning. It was a classic pitching duel. It was very intense. Every play mattered. Every movement had you sitting on the edge of the bench waiting for something to happen. It was two good pitchers battling it out, both wanting to win. When the bottom of the ninth inning came up the score was still tied. My team was up to bat. We had managed to get the bases loaded with three quick singles. From that point on the next two batters had struck out. Then the coach did something that surprised me. He called me over and said, "Get ready, you're pinch hitting."

I just looked at him dumbfounded. My only thoughts were, "Are you kidding me? You do remember that I haven't gotten a hit all year?"

I just said, "Okay."

I grabbed my bat and started to swing it for warm ups. Before I could step up to the plate the manager came over to me and said, "Now is the time for you to show the coach that he made the right decision when he brought you onto this team."

I just looked at him. I had no idea what he was talking about. And right about now I didn't care. I had to go face one of the best pitchers in the league and try to get a hit. And to me that looked like an insurmountable task. Just before stepping into the batters box I looked at the opposing team to see how they were planning on playing me. I had never done this before. It was something that I had seen our good hitters do all the time. All I was trying to do was buy some time to gather my thoughts. I was surprised. They had shifted their team to the right side of the field.

Obviously they were waiting for me to try and pull the ball into that area. I exhaled to relax myself before getting into the batters box.

Now all of sudden it struck me just how large that the opposing pitcher looked standing on the pitcher's mound. He was very intimidating. He looked like a giant standing out there. I knew it was sixty feet away, but right now it looked like he was standing barely ten feet away from me. And he was starting his wind up.

The first pitch came. It was a strike. I was shocked. That ball was extremely fast. I stepped out of the batter's box to gather my thoughts. I kept repeating to myself, "You guys in the field have no idea. I couldn't hit that ball even if I wanted to. And you can forget about pulling that pitch to the right field. It is just too fast for me to even hit it."

The second pitch came. It was a ball. I breathed a little easier. I kept thinking, "Three more pitches like that and I don't have to worry about getting a hit. We would win by the pitcher walking in the winning run." And that would have been okay with me. I wouldn't have to worry about trying to hit one these pitches if that happened.

Unfortunately, things did not work out that way. The next pitch was another strike. I just kept repeating to myself, " If this next pitch is even close I am going to have to swing." The pitch came. I noticed, as soon as it left the pitchers hand, that it might be a strike. As it came towards me it appeared to get larger and larger. It looked like it was going to be a strike. I closed my eyes. I swung the bat as hard and as fast as I could. I felt contact. It made a strange thumping sound. I looked up and to my amazement I saw the ball bouncing over third base. I took off running to first. That ninety feet seemed like it took forever. When I got there everyone on my team was jumping for joy.

I had done it. I hit a single in the one area that no one was covering. With that hit our team had won the championship.

The coach came running over to me and said, "I knew it, I just knew it, you're just one of those guys who do well under pressure. And now you have proven it." He then proceeded to hug me and celebrate with the rest of the team. I felt great. I was a hero. For that moment at least I was not invisible and it felt great. I was on top of the world at that moment. We had won and I had done something to accomplish it. We were now the Babe Ruth city Champions because of that one hit. And I wasn't invisible to anyone.

Doug and I were walking home from that game, which took place a mile from our neighborhood, when Doug said, "Well at least you finally got your first hit. And talk about doing it the hard way."

I just smiled and said, "Yea, it's too bad that it was just luck."

Doug was confused. All he could do was ask, "What do you mean."

I looked at him and said, "When I saw that pitch coming I closed my eyes and swung as hard as I could, and I was lucky that it made it down the third baseline."

Doug just laughed and said: "I guess it's true when they say it is better to be lucky than good."

All that meant was that I had amazed him. And this was his way of letting me know just how much. It was our little game again and we enjoyed it. We both just laughed and walked home.

The First Time

All during this time my father was constantly trying to come up with different ways to help me get through the issues that were still bothering me surrounding the death of the two infants. He had come up with some unique ideas on how to do this. One of the things he did was to teach John and me how to box. Our dad had boxed in the Navy and he had figured that it would be a good thing for us both to learn how to defend ourselves.

Now to me this was fun. I got a chance to beat up my older brother and release some of my emotions at the same time. To me it was a possible winning situation. And I was looking forward to the opportunity.

Unfortunately for me I was wrong. You see I had very fast hands and could hit John twenty to thirty times before he could strike me even once. In fact whenever he got tired of me hitting him, he would just drop his arms to his side and allow me to strike him as often as I wanted to. At first I really liked this part. The only thing wrong was that John would eventually say, " It's my turn." That usually meant that he would raise his left arm and hit me. Just once. And every time he did that I ended up on the floor in a daze. No matter how many times I tried there was no stopping the outcome. I always ended up on the floor with him asking me, with a sheepish grin, "Are you okay little brother."

Needless to say I didn't continue the boxing activity long. I got real tired of kissing the floor whenever John felt like ending the match. This was one thing I didn't mind quitting. At least I would not feel that pain anymore. It didn't do much for my confidence either. All I knew was I didn't want that kind of physical pain anymore.

. Our father came up with one other idea to help me with my emotional issues. This one included me getting a part time job to enable me to take my mind off of everything.

As it turned out my brother, John, had gotten a part time job at a family owned grocery store on Main Street. The owners were friends of my fathers and he thought this might be the right answer for me. So my father spoke to them and they offered me a part time job stocking shelves and helping with the weekly meat truck deliveries. To me this seemed like a good idea, I could earn a few bucks and stay out of the house for a couple of hours a week. The pay wasn't much, but it did give me some spending money. And that part I wasn't complaining about at all. I could always use some spending money. And besides it kept me out of the house. And I didn't have to contend with being invisible as long as I was not there.

The first couple of days were pretty quiet for me. I would bring out the boxes of the stock, find out the price, stamp the items, and place them on the proper shelf, where they went. I didn't always place them correctly, but in time I learned how. The owner's were very patient with me. It took a while but I finally started to catch on. It wasn't that hard after all. It was pretty boring. I just kept reminding myself that it was better than being at home and then I could deal with it. The owner and his wife were great. They were very patient and understanding. I was getting close to them both and I enjoyed their friendship.

. Then one day the meat delivery truck came. I went with John to the back of the store. John explained that the driver would hand us a quarter of a cow and we would bring it into the meat locker where it would be held in storage until it was needed. That didn't sound that hard to me.

Then I watched as the driver put a quarter of a cow on each of my older brother's shoulders and John walked into the store showing little or no effort with them. The whole movement seemed effortless for him.

I looked at that and said to myself, '"It doesn't look like its that hard to do. If John can do it so can I." For some reason I always thought that whatever John could do I was also capable of doing. Call it foolish pride, if you want to, but it was important to me that John recognized that I was his equal.

Well, when the first quarter of a cow was placed on my shoulder I dropped straight to my knees. I had never felt that much weight in my life. I held on to the railing next to me and fought my way to an upright position with my knees shaking all the way. Then the driver asked, "Do you want the other one on your other shoulder now?"

I just looked at him and said, "No, no, this is fine," and I proceeded to slowly walk into the store. To me that was an enormous task. It felt like it was taking me forever. Each step was agony. The amount of effort to move my feet was staggering. The entire way in there, I kept asking myself the same question. " How the hell did John do two of these at a time?" And once again I found myself not being able to compete with my older brother. I just kept asking myself: " Is there anything that he doesn't excel at?" And that usual feeling of despair came back again. Again I had tried to come up with some way to get John to respect me and failed. I sure was getting tired of not being successful at this.

I was happy when that day was over. My shoulders and legs were still sore from that meat delivery experience. My only hope was that it would get easier the more I did it. To this point in my life I had found out that my older brother was better in school than me. And he was definitely stronger than I was. It just seemed that there was nothing that I could do to impress my older brother. After all that is all I really wanted to do. I just wanted John to respect me the way I respected him. John was always fair to me. He went out of his way sometimes to treat me fairly.

The only trouble was I interpreted this activity as him trying to make up for me being the invisible one. And therefore he was coming across to me as feeling sorry for me. That is not what I was after. All I really wanted him to do was to treat me as his equal, not his younger brother.

Early one evening my dad came to me and asked if I wanted to go with him to watch my brother's drum corps compete at the fair grounds. I asked if Doug could come with us and my father said, "Sure," so we all went together.

It turns out that this competition was the Massachusetts State Championships taking place in the Westfield fair grounds. I had been there before and I remembered it as a hot and dusty place. And sure enough it didn't change. It was still a hot and dusty place.

When we got there Doug and I started wandering around. We wanted to check out all of the girls there. After all, the place was filled with thousands of people and some very friendly females. We both had become aware of the opposite sex and we were very interested in learning as much as we could about them. We were especially interested in meeting as many as we possibly could. That day we met quite a few of them. We were having a lot of fun flirting with them. It was clear from the start that they were only willing to flirt with us and nothing else. That fact didn't bother us. We were having fun.

By the time we started back to where my father was he was walking towards us. As he came towards us he said, "You just missed your brother's drum corps, they are coming off the stand now."

From his tone you could tell that he was not angry. But you could definitely tell that he was frustrated that we were not there to see it.

Missing my brother's drum corps didn't bother me at all. After all I had really only gone to see if I could meet some girl and to have fun. But then I saw something coming towards me that held me in complete amazement.

It was a group carrying rifles and flags that I could not believe. They were dressed in black uniforms with white shoes and white gloves. Their pants had a bright yellow stripe down the side. The jacket was waist length with gold circus piping on their sleeves and a large brass button in the center of the piping. The same circus piping was on their chest with similar large brass buttons in the center of the piping. On their chest was a gold breastplate with a black falcon imprinted on it. It mesmerized you. It was the only thing that you could see. That gold breastplate with the black polish falcon on it was something that you just couldn't take your eyes of off. And the closer they came the more in awe of them I became.

They wore black military style hats with very shiny brims and a feathery yellow plume sat on the top of the hat. I couldn't help myself; I just stood there with my mouth wide open staring at this group coming towards me. They kept coming until they were even with me. From this vantage point I could see clearly how precise they were. They wore white gloves on their hands and whenever their left arms came forward they would swing them towards their faces, stopping just short of their noses. Each and every one of them executed this movement flawlessly. All of their arms went to the exact same height at the exact same time. They continued marching past me while my mouth hung open.

I found myself walking along with this group and I was amazed by their precision. Every step they took, they took as one. Every arm swing with the left arm going up to their face they did so as one. Their timing was perfect. To me it was beautiful.

When they stopped I heard my brother call me, 'Hey Mike, what did you think". I had to explain to him that I had missed their performance. I did tell him that our father thought it was great. He did look a little disappointed. That didn't bother me. I was too concerned about the group I had just seen.

The only thing I wanted to know from him was who were those guys were out in front of the drum corps. John then explained to me that they were the color guard for the drum corps. And they were the best. They had won the last four Northeastern titles. I just looked at them. As they broke ranks I noticed something. I turned to Doug and said, "I know some of those guys, and they are in my class at school."

Doug responded by saying that he knew a couple of them too. Right then and there I decided that I had to talk to them when school started to find out more about this group. I was amazed that I knew someone that could perform in such a way. They also surprised Doug. He just didn't know how to respond to the fact that he knew someone marching with that group. And for once he could not come up with an obnoxious comment for the occasion. That fact alone impressed me.

Fall

The summer was coming to a close now. I was still working part time at the grocery store. I had finally managed to carry a quarter of a cow without falling down. And as far as I was concerned, I was never even going to attempt carrying two like my brother John did.

All during the rest of the summer, I was constantly asking my brother about the color guard. I wanted to know how they did in competitions and especially how my classmates did. I couldn't wait for school to start so I could talk to them about it. John was very patient with me. He would respond by telling me that the color guard had won again and leave it at that. Instead of saying anymore about the subject he would just say: " I have to go do my homework now. Don't you have any to do?" I usually didn't bother answering that question I just walked away. This was John's method of getting even with me. He would only use this line when he really didn't want to answer my questions. He knew this approach normally put me into a defensive mode and consequently I would just walk away from him.

My opinion of school at that time was basically very low. After all, attending a catholic grammar school and a catholic high school definitely had its drawbacks. For one thing, there was no physical education program in existence in our school. Instead all they focused on was academics. Not my favorite activity. And the way the nuns did it you had to accomplish a lot of work to accomplish anything. And that was something that I was not going to have anything to do with.

My older brother John, as it turns out was very smart and studious. He always accomplished all of his homework on time. And he did all of his assignments. And needless to say the nuns enjoyed having him in their classes. You have to understand that all through my grammar school years the nun's kept asking me, "Why can't you be like your older brother?"

My usual answer to this question was, "I am not my brother."

Needless to say, this response did not sit well with the nuns of St. Mary's school. However, they had made a grave error with me. They had told me that homework was worth 15% of my total grade, class participation was worth 10% of my grade, and the mid-term and final tests would equate to being worth 75% of my total grade for a class. An average of 70% was required for a student to advance to the next grade level.

That was all I needed to hear. From then on homework and class participation were out. The only thing I had to be concerned about was mid-term and final exams.

This decision resulted in multiple visits to the principal's office and multiple calls to my mother, who did not appreciate having to leave my two younger brothers at home to come to the school and deal with these issues.

Needless to say I always got an ear full when I got home. And again I would hear the same words from my mother that I was growing to hate. Namely the usual question of: "Why can't you be like your brother?"

And she would get the same answer as the Nuns. The only trouble is it doesn't work so well with your mother. She usually just looked at me and said: " You are more than capable of doing whatever you decide to do. So start doing something.

And I don't appreciate having to leave your brothers with a baby sitter just to hear that you haven't done you homework again. You know I don't like leaving them with anyone. Its about time you grew up." The conversation usually ended with her telling me that she did not want to have to go to the school for that subject again. Her comments usually made me feel very small for making her leave my brothers with a baby sitter while she attended to my issues. I had to amend my plan. I didn't like feeling small in my mother's eyes. And that often resulted in me doing just enough homework to stop my mother from paying a weekly visit to the school.

It really surprised me just how well this little plan of mine worked out. I was passing all of his class with little or no work being done.

One of the things that I did enjoy was visiting with my classmates. I guess you would call me a social person. I would rather talk to my classmates than do homework any day of the week. On many occasions I would talk to Billy and Robert, the two members of the drum corps color guard that I had seen during the summer. Robert, as it turned out was the color guard sergeant, or the leader. Namely, he was the person in charge of all the movements of the color guard. He was about Two inches shorter than I was and the fact that he was the leader of that group impressed me. Billy on the other hand was only an inch shorter than I was and he was a flag carrier in the color guard.

Billy and Robert were very patient with my questions. I wanted to know everything I could about the group. I was really surprised how Robert seemed embarrassed at the questions I was asking. I just thought to myself, if I were a member of a group like that I would be screaming about it. I just didn't understand his response. After all the color guard I had seen was simply outstanding.

I knew that if I was part of that organization I would be extremely proud of it. And I would also not be afraid to let the world know how good they were.

As they were talking one day Billy and Robert mentioned that they were going to form a color guard for the High School band and they wanted to know if I wanted to try out for it. My response was " *DEFINITELY.*"

So we all met in the basement after school for the tryouts. Billy and Robert tried to teach people how to do a right face and a left face movement and keep there heals and toes in the correct positions.

I found out rather quickly that this was not an easy thing to do, so I struggled to get it right. It seemed that no matter what I did I couldn't get the timing with the other people right. Robert kept trying to work with me. It took a couple of weeks but I finally got it. Talk about feeling uncoordinated, that was me. And yet I had done it. I had accomplished something that was very important to me and it felt great.

Unfortunately, after about three weeks of tryouts they had to make a decision. Robert came to me to tell me that I was not going to make it into the High School color guard. This was a let down, but I couldn't let anyone know just how depressed I was about it. It felt like the rug had just been pulled out from underneath me. After all I had missed a chance to march with Billy and Robert. Just to have marched with them would have been exciting to me. And I felt embarrassed about my feeble attempt to accomplish what they had tried to teach me. The words that my mother had constantly used kept coming back to me. Namely: "You can accomplish whatever you put your mind to." Well, I t had tried this using her way and again I was embarrassed at the outcome. It seemed like no matter how hard I tried I was destined to be invisible.

I still remembered seeing Robert and Billy in the drum corps color guard and I was impressed at what they could do. So once again I drove my emotions inward and hoped that no one would ever see them. It was embarrassing for me. I had failed at something I really wanted to do. And the last thing I wanted was for someone to see that emotion. I didn't hang around with Robert or Billy very much after that. It was too much of a reminder of my embarrassment to be around them.

About four weeks later Billy came up to me and told me that the local drum corps color guard was looking for new members and asked if I wanted to join. I jumped at the chance and asked when and where. Billy told me that the practice was at 7:00 PM on Thursday and he would meet me at the corner of Franklin and Washington Street about 6:30 PM to show me where the practice was being held. I agreed to be there.

Billy was on time. He was surprised that I was there, and on time. We walked together along Washington Street while Billy explained the different members of the color guard. Robert, the color guard sergeant, I already knew, so Billy started talking about the Grover brothers from West Springfield.

He started off by saying that they take the bus over from West Springfield every week. And they had to leave the practices exactly at nine pm in order to catch the last bus home. He then explained that there were four of them. There was Bobby, who was a rifleman in the guard and had been marching for a couple of years. According to Billy his eyes light up whenever he smiles or whenever he was in uniform, There was his brother

Dick, who was Bobby's twin, was also a rifleman and had been marching for a couple of years. He also enjoyed marching in the color guard.

And according to Billy he really enjoyed life itself, there was Gary, the middle brother, who had joined the same time as Billy and he was carrying a flag. According to Billy, was a little more serious than the other two but loved being part of the color guard. And then there was Danny, the youngest brother, who was new to the color guard and according to Billy had to tryout just like I did.

My response was swift, "What do mean tryout? I thought I was just coming to join. Don't you remember what happened with the high school color guard?"

All I could think of was my failure at trying out for the High School color guard. I had no intention of going through that again. I didn't care what he said. I was not going through that again.

Billy spent the rest of the walk calming me down, explaining that it would be worth it. "Just try it," was all he would say. He just kept repeating it all the way there. I finally agreed to try it. All the while in the back of my mind I was thinking," If I even get a hint of this coming out like the try outs for the High School color guard I am out of here." I was willing to try it. I was not willing to feel that embarrassment again. I didn't care what anybody said. That was not going to be part of my life again.

PART TWO

The First Practice

As we continued walking, Billy explained that there were two other Drum Corps in town that they competed against, and I should not be surprised if they showed up at our practices to watch us. I was surprised. I only knew of this Drum Corps. I was impressed that there were others that existed in our town. And to be told that they came to their practices to watch was a concept that was completely foreign to me. There was only one reason I could think of that an opposing color guard would come to their practices. That was that they must have been looking for some way to beat them on the competition field. And if that was the case I was thoroughly impressed.

When we turned the corner of School Street where the VFW (Veterans of Foreign Wars) hall was, Billy explained that the building with the people in front of it was our destination.

There in front of the VFW hall was a group of about eight people. Among them was my older brother John. As Billy and I approached John came out to meet us, with his trumpet case in his hand, and asked, "What are you doing here little brother?"

I just looked at him and said, "I'm going to tryout for the color guard."

John's only response was, "Okay. But there is one thing you have to remember. These guys don't take the easy way out. They don't fool around. They are very serious about what they do. And you don't exactly have a very good track record of completing things that you have to work at. So if you are not going to be serious about this, you shouldn't do it."

I could tell that he doubted my intentions for being there. I guess I couldn't blame him. He was very familiar with my past experiences. And he was trying to warn me that my past habit of quitting anything that was difficult for me was not going to be acceptable in this case. I resented his presumption that I would not be able to follow up on this one. I was embarrassed that he would even say these things in front of other people. In my mind he should have waited until we got home to discuss this. Of course if he did I would probably ignore him. So I guess he did have a right to say something after all. I just looked at my older brother and said to myself, "Who knows? I might even like it. After all I am just here to see what it is all about."

When we got to the front of the building Billy introduced me to everyone. First there were the four Grover brothers. Bobby, who stood about six feet tall with a muscular build and dark brown hair. When he shook my hand there was a warm smile and a twinkle in his eye that just made me feel that he was genuinely happy to meet me. Next was his brother Dick, who stood about six feet with a muscular build with brown hair and some freckles. He also gave me that feeling of genuine warmth when I met him. The brother named Gary was next, he was about my height, medium build and black hair combed after in a style similar to Elvis Presley. And when I shook his hand he had a wry smirk on his face and nodded towards me. Then there was Danny; he stood about an inch shorter than me, with a medium build and brown hair like his brother Dick. When I was introduced to Danny I found myself saying, "I understand that we are both here to tryout for the color guard tonight."

Danny just smiled and said, "We sure are." His smile was warm and friendly. I felt comfortable with him right away. He just felt like someone that I would enjoy getting to know.

The next person I met was an older man named Eddie; he was about my height with dark hair and a medium build. And Billy introduced him as the color guard instructor. The only other person there was Robert. And I said, "At least I know you."

Robert responded by saying, "That is only because we went through grammar school together." He was being sarcastic and I knew it.

After all he and I did go through grammar school together. We really didn't know each other that well. We lived about two miles apart and had each focused on our own friendships we had developed in our respective neighborhoods to this point. I guess you could define our relationship as acquaintances through school.

Then Eddie said, "It's time. Lets all go inside and get this practice started."

We all went into the building. Once we got inside, I noticed a large open hall with a stairway leading downward on the left side of the room. Everyone headed for that stairway, so I followed them down the stairs.

When we got down the stairs we were in a room with beige walls about eight feet wide and ten feet long. On the right wall was another door. They all went through the door so I followed them. The second room was a lot larger than the first. It was about twenty feet wide and thirty feet long with dark paneling along the walls.

Once we were inside the second room Eddie asked all of the new people to line up in a straight line. It turns out that there were four of us. And I sheepishly joined the others standing along the line that he had indicated. Eddie then told Gary and Billy to join us. And they did. Then he asked Robert to close the door and he did. Eddie started the practice with the following speech. He started by saying, "Before we get started I have few things that I need to explain to everyone. First of all if you are not here to tryout for the Whip City Drum Corps Color Guard you need to leave now."

At this point Robert, Bobby, Dick, and another person named Ray started to move towards the door. Eddie just shot them a very stern look and said, "You guys better not be going anywhere."

The four of them just smiled and went back to their places. Eddie then continued with his talk. "The second thing I want to cover is that door. What I mean is that if you have an ego, you leave it on the other side of that door when you are here. There is no room for egos in this color guard. Whatever one of us does affects all of us. And thirdly, we have some simple rules in this drum corps: No drinking alcohol, no fighting, and no drugs are allowed at any time. If you are found doing any of these, you will be dismissed from the corps immediately without question. If you cannot live by these rules I suggest you leave now."

I had to look around. Not a soul moved. I had to think about this. What this person named Eddie was saying was that I could no longer take part in some of the things that I had learned to enjoy if I was around these guys during drum corps. I was embarrassed to think that I almost left at that point. Just thinking about those rules made me feel like I was joining the military. But I didn't want to be the only one walking out. So I stayed. I just kept thinking," if I don't like it I can just quit." Now that was something that I was good at.

Eddie did explain that normally they practiced for two hours a week on Thursday's and those who smoked would get a break after the first hour of practice. Then he said," Robert, Bobby, Dick, and Ray will work with you guys as we get started."

Eddie then told everyone that they were going to start with the position of attention. Robert then gave the command, "Attention." On this command all of us new people moved to what we considered the correct position for this command.

Eddie then explained that he wanted everyone to look straight ahead, with their stomachs in, their chests out and their chins in. Then Eddie, Bobby, Dick, and Ray all went around showing everyone where their fingers should be placed and how their feet should be positioned. He kept pointing out that our heels should be even and straight. Our toes should be even. And our feet need to be at a forty-five degree angle. Along with this our hands should be at our sides with our thumbs on one side of the seam of our pants. Along with all of your fingers being cupped in order for all of them to touch your pant legs. You could tell right away that Eddie, Bobby, and Dick were very familiar with doing this. Ray was a little apprehensive while he was helping people. All the time while this was going on, Eddie kept saying, "Don't worry about getting anything we do tonight perfect namely because we are going to continue doing these things until you cannot get them wrong."

I thought to myself: " I have heard that statement before. John always says it about practicing the scale on his trumpet. He has got to be kidding. There is no way that we can continue doing this until we can't get it wrong. That is just not possible."

Then, on Eddie's cue Robert gave the command for left face.
And once again the training group went around showing
everyone how to perform the movement so their feet ended up
in the perfect position. This command is executed by lifting your
left toe, while lifting your right heal, pushing with your right toe
so you pivot on you left heal until your body is ninety degrees
from your starting point And on Eddie's cue Robert then gave
the command for right face. In order to accomplish this you lift
your left heal, and your right toe, push with your left toe, and
pivot on you right heal until you are ninety degrees from your
starting point And the training from the others continued with
these same moves.

Fortunately, I remembered all of this from when Robert
had tried to teach me earlier in the school year so this part
was coming easy for me. After about ten minutes of these
commands, Eddie came over to me and asked me if I had any
training because I was doing really well.

I didn't know to respond at first. I was confused. Why would
someone with this much knowledge be asking me this question?
So without thinking I responded with the only answer that
came into my head," No". Immediately after saying that I knew
that it was wrong but I couldn't take it back now. The practice
continued on like this for about forty-five minutes. Then Eddie
said, " Let's take a break."

We all headed outside for a smoke. When we got to the top
of the stairs I saw that the room was filled with about forty
people all holding musical instruments. My brother was sitting
on a chair and nodded to me when I saw him. I responded with
a nod. This was supposed to be a message to my older brother.
I was trying to say, "Yes, I am still here. And I am going to try
this color guard thing to see if it is something that I want to
do."

When we got outside I commented as to the number of people in there. Eddie just looked at me and asked, "Do you know any of them."

I just looked at him and said, "One of those trumpet players is my older brother."

Eddie's response was, "Then you must be John's younger brother."

I replied, "I am. And I am surprised that he is in this Drum corps. The only thing I have ever heard him play on his trumpet is the scale."

Eddie just laughed and explained that every new musical member of the Drum corps usually starts out as the best in their high school but when they get to drum Corps they find out that they are considered mediocre at best. Fortunately the corps music director had the ability to get the best out of all of them. About this time Robert came over to Eddie and asked if he could talk to him. Eddie just turned to the others and said, "Finish up your smokes and come back in so we can get started again."

After Eddie left me I turned to the others and said, "He is not kidding about this practice until you can't get it wrong thing is he?"

Gary responded very quickly with, " Nope, that's Eddie."

When we all went back inside Eddie and Robert were standing together. Eddie then asked me to join them for a minute. When I got over to them Eddie asked, "Mike, according to Robert he has trained you in the past, did you lie to me earlier?"

I found myself embarrassed and I didn't know how to respond at first. My face was turning red and I could feel it. And for the first time in a while I was scared. I had been caught and there was no way out of it. I decided to tell the truth. "Yes, I did lie to you, I didn't think of it until after I said it but Robert did teach me.

And by the way, Robert, you did a great job with it. I am sorry Robert especially since you had to be so patient with me in the first place."

Eddie just looked at me, I could tell that he just knew how embarrassed I was, by the shade of red on my face, and he said, "Okay, we are going to let you stay with the color guard under one condition. And before I tell you what that is you have to remember that you have to earn the trust of every one of these guys and I am not sure that Robert is comfortable with you right now, even though you have apologized to him. The condition is that there can be no more lies. Do you agree?"

I looked at him. I had to think about it. Was this something I really wanted to do? That question kept running through my mind. The answer that I kept coming up with was for now I do. So I agreed with him. Eddie just smiled and said, "Okay let's get back to practice."

We continued practicing the same things we had done for the first hour. I could feel the redness in my face going away slowly as we practiced. A certain thought kept running through my head. First of all it was important that I didn't lie to these people again. Secondly I wanted to know when we had gotten to the point where we could no longer do the moves wrong. It was getting old and boring to me.

That first practice was over and all the way home I just talked about it with my older brother John. I didn't tell John about my lying, but I did tell him how Eddie was insistent on us practicing something until we couldn't get it wrong. I was still amazed by that concept. John didn't react much to my concerns. He just shrugged his shoulders and said: " That's just the way Eddie is." His response was almost the exact words that Gary had used to respond to the same question.

I really was starting to wonder about this group. As far as I was concerned they had a strange concept of how to practice something.

On the way home John informed me of what he knew about the members of the color guard. He had spent the last summer marching with this group and he felt that he had gotten to know them during that experience. According to him, Bobby was a very outgoing person who loved life and enjoyed being with people, and whenever he spoke people listened to him because he was respected all throughout drum corps. Everyone also respected his brother, Dick. He was however, an introverted type of person who only spoke when he had something to say. Gary was similar to Dick with a strong love of life. Danny, according to John was similar to Bobby, even though he looked like Dick. I was impressed with John's analysis of the four brothers. The more I thought about it, the more I believed that my older brother had completely described them to a tee. I just couldn't figure out how my brother did that so accurately. I had a new level of respect for him after that. I couldn't believe how insightful his observations were. But I wasn't going to tell him. At least not yet, I was going to save that feeling for another time.

John also kept asking me if I was coming back next week for practice. My only response to him was, " Let's wait and see what next Thursday brings." He didn't like my response. He wanted an answer right away. And in my own defense I wasn't sure at that point. It all seemed like too much work to me. To practice until you couldn't do something wrong just came across as a waste of time to me. That whole concept bothered me. I just couldn't get it out of my head.

I couldn't wait to get home and talk to Doug about the events of the practice. I wasn't sure how Doug would respond. I just needed to talk to someone about the concept.

All during the following school week Billy kept asking me if I was going to go with him to the next practice. At first I wasn't sure. By Wednesday of that week I made a decision. Basically, it was that I would go to the next practice and try it again.

After all I didn't have anything else to do on Thursday nights except homework and I wasn't going to do that.

The next practice went a little easier for me. We did continue to practice the same things, but they were coming easier to me now. Not being embarrassed made a big difference in my attitude. Consequently I decided to continue going. I was having fun during the breaks and these guys were very interesting to be around and a lot of fun. And besides that they even seemed happy to see me there. And I liked that. I wasn't invisible and it felt good. It felt real good being accepted. And what was even better they respected me and I respected them.

Until You Can't Get It Wrong

For the next couple of Thursday's, we continued to practice the same things we had learned the first week. I kept asking myself the same question. "When do we learn something else?" Going over the same thing over and over again was getting a bit old to me, and my patience was starting to wear real thin about how practical this concept was.

During the breaks I would always ask the others the same question. Unfortunately, I always got the same answer. "Until we can't get it wrong."

Then one Thursday evening when we arrived for practice something different happened. Eddie handed each one of the new people a round pole with threads on one end about five feet in length. He then proceeded to explain that these were half of the flagpoles that the color guard carried, and we were going to start learning the flag manual.

Needless to say I was happy. Finally we were going to get to learn something else. This half of a flagpole came up to my shoulder. I just looked at it and said to myself: "This is only half of it. I wonder what the whole flagpole is like."

Eddie then handed us each a white leather strap with a belt like adjustment and white cup in the middle of it. He explained that these were the flag cups. The next thing he said made me listen very intently. Eddie explained the following; "These flag cups should fit you so they are at waist height. Any lower and you might not be able to have children in the future." (Giggle, giggle)

That part I was listening to. I was going to make sure that the flag cup was worn in the correct position.

From that point on Robert worked with us, teaching us flag manual while the rest of the color guard practiced their rifle manual. Again I was impressed with Robert's knowledge. He took the time with each person to explain where each finger was supposed to be for every movement, as well as how all of the flags had to be held at the same height and angle all of the time. No matter what we did, our timing was way off. Consequently, he just kept going over each move. I was starting to feel the pressure of trying to get it consistently right. It definitely was not easy. And suddenly Robert started counting for every move we made. As he was doing this he kept saying, " Remember this cadence. This is how you're going to have to perform these moves with the flag in order to keep your timing together."

My only response was a question I kept repeating to myself. " How in the world can counting together while we are doing these moves help us at all?"

To my surprise it worked. By the end of the first half of practice we had improved our timing to the point where we could get two moves on the flag without any negative comments from Robert. This was a massive improvement for me and I really enjoyed it.

During the second half of practice Eddie came back into the room where we were working on our flag manual. He just stood there and watched for a few minutes. Then he spoke and said, "Once you learn this you will practice it every week for the first half of each practice. I also want you to take turns giving commands and teaching each other what you are doing wrong. We will start this next week with Gary starting off as the leader for that practice. The week after that Billy will take over and you will all gets a chance to try it out."

I was amazed and I couldn't wait for my chance to lead this group. Before Eddie left the room I asked him, "And how long do you expect us to practice like this?"

As soon as I asked the question I knew the answer. All Eddie did was smile and say, "Until you can't get it wrong."

Now this concept of all of us taking turns leading the practice sounded interesting to me. I soon learned that it was more than just a chance to lead the group. It was an opportunity to show what we had learned. We all took turns doing this. And every time someone new was doing this they always found some minor adjustments that were required to improve the timing of the flag manual. The changes I made were simple enough. Danny was mouthing the count while he was doing the manual. It was very easy for me to point that out to him and remind him that he should only count to himself. I was surprised how quickly the timing of the flag manual became second nature to us. If a command was called we no longer needed to count to get the timing. It was coming naturally to us. We were becoming a group that moved and thought like one. And this was only the beginning of my learning experience.

The other half of each practice from then on was the whole guard going through our paces on flag and rifle manual together. It was during the first of these practice sessions that Eddie set the color guard line up according to height. At the right end he placed Bobby, then Ray, and then myself. After me were the other flags, with Gary and Dick at the left end. It was at this time Eddie mentioned to me that I was always going to be carrying the American flag, and it was a great honor. And that part felt good to me. I had an important job in this color guard. I was beginning to feel proud about my newfound status.

Then Dick chimed in with, "And besides that you are the tallest one in the flag line." I had grown to about six feet and stood taller than the other members of the flag line. I was happy, that I had a definite place. What's even better I had the easiest of all of the flags to work with. To me this might just work out. In the color guard the American flag never salutes, and I only had to hold it up against my nose. I didn't have to worry about flag angles or saluting. This looked like it was right up my alley. I could get away with doing the manual and having the easy way out.

After about two months of practicing this way, Eddie put a new twist into our routine. When we got to practice one day he met us with rifles. Not the chrome plated type that the color guard normally carried, But Springfield 1903 model weapons. He handed each member one of these and said, "Hold on to this for a minute while I explain what we are doing."

These rifles were a lot heavier than I thought. I guess when you watch someone perform rifle manual, and it seems effortless, you get the impression that they are light. And that was definitely not the case.

Eddie then held up a book and said, "This book is the FM22-5, and it is the military manual used to teach people what is expected of them with a rifle as well as the correct drill and ceremony procedures while they are in the Army. It is also what Drum Corps judges use in order to judge competitors. You will all get one of these. Before we get through you will know it from cover to cover. And we will test you on your knowledge of this book."

It was about this point that I said to myself, " Say what! You want me to learn what? This is beginning to sound and awful lot like homework and I don't do that." Eddie just smiled at me.

Then he held up a sheet of paper and said, "This is the individual rifle sheet that is used in competition. There are 21 commands on it. Before we are through you will be able to perform each one of these proficiently as an individual and as a unit. Bobby, Dick, and Robert are going to start working with all of you on your individual rifle manual. And in three weeks Robert and I are going to use these sheets to judge you individually."

I just looked at him and said to myself, "You have got to be kidding me. With my lack of ability to learn this stuff, you really expect me to learn it in a couple of weeks?"

So they started. Bobby was stuck with working with me. It is a good thing that he was a patient person. By the end of practice that night I was beginning to understand where each finger was suppose to be for each movement. I was still trying to grasp how to hold the rifle level to the ground on certain positions. That was not getting through to me at all. On the way home Billy and I talked. I was concerned. This rifle manual stuff was too much like homework to me, and I just didn't do that. After all I didn't want to take any responsibility for actions unless I had to. I had gotten away with this attitude so far, and it was becoming quite comfortable for me. Billy suggested that maybe we could get together after school one day a week and practice together.

He also said that his grandfather had some rifles they could use for practice. I thought about it, and decided that maybe with his help I could do this. So we agreed to do this every Tuesday afternoon from then on. This whole activity was definitely against my better judgment. It meant that I might have to take responsibility for my actions.

I rationalized it to myself by saying," At least with Billy's help I might just be able to do something with this project." So I agreed to try it. I t couldn't hurt.

When the time came for Eddie and Robert to do the judging I was feeling pretty confident. I had learned the rifle manual and, with Billy's help, and as far as I was concerned, I wasn't bad at it. This attitude was all well and good until I watched Gary and Danny going through the sheet with Eddie and Robert. They were great. And all of a sudden I felt like I was in trouble. I new right then and there that I didn't have a chance competing against them. My turn came, and I was nervous.

As Robert called the commands I did them and Eddie judged them. I could feel my hands and arms shaking as I performed each movement. This was scary to say the least.

After everyone had completed this task Eddie called all of us into the room. He just stood there. I had all kinds of things running through his mind. "Am I out because I didn't do well?" Those were the thoughts running through my head. If they had decided that I wasn't good enough all that practicing with Billy would have been worthless. And that is about how I would have felt if that was the outcome.

Eddie just calmly said, "You all did well, it is obvious to us that you had to work together to accomplish what we saw and I am proud of you. Guess what, we are going to continue practicing with these rifles. And guess how long we are going to do it."

In unison the whole guard said, "Until we can't do it wrong."

When I got home that night I talked to Doug about this philosophy. Doug's response was short and to the point, "It sounds like too much work."

Then I proceeded to explain it to him. I amazed myself with how much I understood the concept. It scared me a little.

I was starting to understand this "until you can't do it wrong" concept. It basically meant that you would work at it until you understood any slight implication towards doing the moves wrong and corrected it prior to completing it. This was something new for me. Understanding the direction things were going prior to their completion was something that I had never considered before. At this point I still wasn't sure if this was a good thing or not. The only thing I knew was that I wanted to continue learning this system that impressed me so much, regardless of what the outcome might be.

Spring Practice

From that point on all of the practices were similar. We would spend the first hour practicing with the flags and the rifles as individual units to improve our timing, and the second hour was spent with the whole color guard working with our assigned equipment to prepare for the upcoming competition season. Then when the snow was melted and the weather was getting warmer Eddie took us outside to practice. This outside practice took place in the adjoining parking lot to the VFW hall on School Street.

Don't get me wrong. The snow was definitely gone from the ground, but the winter wind was still present, and it was howling at about twenty miles an hour. This was the first time we had the complete flags attached to our flagpoles, and what a difference that made. I couldn't get over it. The flagpole was a total of ten feet tall and had a full four-foot by five-foot flag, with double thickness, attached to it. On top of that each flag had a flat-bronzed spear tip attached to it that had to remain flat at all times. And that wind would just blow you around everywhere. It would jerk your whole body from side to side whenever it was present. Unfortunately for me, my flag had an eagle attached to it that had to be kept straight all of the time.

Eddie just kept repeating the same thing over and over again, " Hold onto to those flag poles. You have to learn to control them in all kinds of weather. Keep them still."

I just couldn't believe how difficult that was. My hand was freezing up against that metal flagpole and that wind just kept moving me around. During our break I spent the whole time trying to warm my hand up.

All during that practice we just stayed at the position of right shoulder. It is accomplished by having the back of your right hand, while grasping the pole, facing you, with your elbow up so your forearm was parallel to the ground. All this was done with the flag being held at a thirty-degree angle from you body. While you were carrying that flag in this position your left arm was constantly swinging in time with everyone else. And if the wind was blowing away from you, you held onto the flagpole with your thumb and your fingertips. If it was against you, your body weight was needed to continue holding it in the correct position. I would have given anything if Robert had called the command for left shoulder. My right arm felt like it was going to fall off.

Eventually we managed to start controlling the flags, wind and all. It felt good to me. It was hard work and I was starting to get the physical strength to accomplish it. At first it didn't seem to me like it was reasonable to carry this size of a flag. The more I thought about it, the more I rationalized it by saying," If you're going to do something, you might as well do it right." Eddie had taught me something in those practices, and I was surprised. I was learning the worth of hard work. As much as I had always fought it in the past, it was beginning to make sense to me now. I felt the difference. And it felt good.

Eddie had also taught us how to take care of each piece of equipment and told us that we were responsible for its condition. Just what I didn't want to hear about at this time, responsibility! All my life I had managed to dodge anything that I had to take responsibility for. And to this point I had been completely successful in doing so.

And now it was made very clear to me that if I wanted to continue being a part of the color guard I had to take part in this activity. So I guess it made sense to me to continue learning whatever Eddie was going to teach us.

That included being responsible for my own equipment. And for once I had something that I was taking responsibility for that I didn't mind doing. What impressed me even more was that I was good at it. Even taking care of the equipment.

One advantage of practicing outside was that the drum corps came out also, and when they marched and played their music it was fantastic. You could feel each note just reverberating through your body. The snare drums and the base drums playing together just made you want to march. You could feel each beat resounding throughout your body. I loved it. There were always extra people there when we practiced. They would just stand and watch, as we would go through our paces. I didn't think much of the people being there until one Thursday night during a break something unusual happened.

As soon as Eddie gave the guard a break he, Bobby, and Dick went over to some people that were watching. At first I didn't think much of that until I noticed that it appeared that Bobby and Dick were teaching them how to do a correct left and right face. This confused me. I turned and asked Billy and Gary, "Who are those people? And why does it look like Bobby and Dick are teaching them?"

Gary responded very quickly. "It looks like they are teaching them because they are. And for your information they are members of a color guard that we compete against in Connecticut."

I was astonished. The only thing he could say was, "Say what?"

Bobby and Dick were on their way back now. I walked over to meet them. I had to know something. As they approached I asked them, "Is it true that they are some of our competition? And if they are, why are you guys teaching them?"

Bobby answered very quickly. "Yes they are our competition, and they asked for our help."

Again I was amazed. I had to ask, "Aren't you afraid that with you helping them they might be able to beat us?"

Dick just laughed and said, "First of all if they improve from what we are doing with them it only means that we, our color guard, has to be better. And secondly, I wouldn't worry about it too much; they only practice until they get it right. And how long do we practice something?"

I just put my hand up and said, "Say no more. Until we can't get it wrong."

When I got home that night Doug was waiting for me. He wanted to know what happened at practice. He was always curious about how the practices went. I had tried to talk him into joining but he would have nothing to do with it.

His response was always the same," Too much like work."

When I told him the story of our competitors coming to practice and being taught by Bobby and Dick he could not believe it. He was completely surprised by the whole thing.

He just kept repeating, " You mean you guys teach your competition? How do you expect to win if you keep doing that?"

My response to him was the same one that was given to me by Bobby and Dick, " This way we have to ensure that we are better than them." Even after saying it myself it really didn't sink in. It still seemed like a strange way to compete to me. But at this point I was willing to try it.

The Season

Then one Thursday night, at the beginning of May, Eddie called the color guard inside. He just stood there with what looked liked uniforms to me. He handed me, Danny, and the other new members each a pair of pants and said, "Try these on. You will need a pair of suspenders. Do not get the ones with clasps; you need suspenders with buttons to attach to these pants. And you better make sure that they are strong suspenders."

While I was trying on the pants I noticed a few things about them. First of all they were heavy wool. Needless to say that did not impress me. Besides the weight, the idea of being able to move around in them bothered me. Then I noticed that they were supposed to be worn just above the waist. To me this was awkward. It felt like they were being worn up around my throat. Then I noticed the buttons for the suspenders and understood why Eddie had said what he did. The suspenders were going to be taking the weight of the pants off of us. This made sense to me. Now I understood how we were going to able to march with them on. They still seemed a little to heavy to march in to me.

Danny and I were excited. "Does this mean we made it?" was the only question out of our mouths.

Eddie just smiled and said, "Yes, you have. We are going to have a ten-man color guard this year and you guys are all part of it. That means that there will be 5 people carrying flags, four rifleman, and Robert out in front as the color guard Sergeant."

Danny and I were so happy that we hugged each other and gave each other a high five-hand clap. Now we couldn't wait to try on the uniforms.

We were out of our minds with excitement. For me it was especially important. This was the first time that I had actually succeeded in doing something I really wanted to do. I just looked at the pants, with a very pleased feeling inside me, before I tried them on. And what do you know the pants fit. They felt good and comfortable.

Then Eddie told us that we had to buy special shoes called white bucks and at least ten pairs of white gloves, and they had to be purchased before the end of the month. This news didn't bother me. I still had that part time job at the grocery store after school, and I had even saved up a few dollars. My older brother, John, had warned me that I might need it if I made the color guard, and sure enough I did. And I was still happy about it.

Then Eddie handed each one of the new members a jacket. When I grabbed mine I could not believe how much it weighed. I said, "This thing feels like it weighs ten pounds." It was hard for me to imagine wearing such a heavy jacket.

Eddie's response was, "It is a heavy wool uniform. And there is a very thick lining. When you wear these you need to wear a short sleeve sweatshirt underneath them. If you don't the lining will cut you all up. And I suggest you get more that one sweatshirt, because we have a lot of days when we have more than one activity planned. Having a dry sweatshirt will be very critical to your ability to continue marching.

The second part of his statement didn't mean much to me at the time. I was only concerned about the weight of the jacket. I couldn't understand how anyone could march with this thing on. And suddenly I found myself thinking of my meager savings account.

What all this meant to me was that my savings were now spent.

I would just have to be careful in my spending for the next couple of weeks if I wanted to march with this color guard. And as far as I was concerned I wanted to march with them. And I was determined that I was going to do whatever it took to accomplish this.

Then Eddie handed us all hats and plumes and told us that we are responsible for their condition. Namely, if the hat brim is not shinny or the plume has lost its feathers we would not be allowed to march with guard until it was fixed or replaced. Fortunately he also explained how we were to maintain the shiny brim and the feathered plume. I took one look at this equipment and decided that I did not want to pay for the replacement of any of it. It just looked too expensive to me. Besides that my savings would already be spent getting the other items I needed.

Eddie then informed us that we needed to purchase a uniform bag to keep the uniforms in and we needed to get the uniforms dry cleaned before the end of the month. In fact he wanted to get the uniforms dry-cleaned after each drum corps activity.

All I could think of was, " Well at least I know where my next couple of pay checks are going."

Once this was done Eddie told us to go upstairs for a meeting with the rest of the Drum Corps. When we got upstairs the director of the Corps, named Jack, was speaking. He stood about two inches shorter than me. He was a stocky man with a short crew cut for a hairstyle and when he spoke everyone in the drum corps listened. He had just handed out uniforms to the new members of the drum corps and was explaining to them how they had to care for them. He then started talking about the upcoming season.

He said, "Our summer has been completely scheduled out. What that means is that we are going to be busy every weekend until October.

There are some days where we have multiple activities so be ready to move quickly when we have to. As an example, we have three parades scheduled for Memorial Day.

And we have to be on time for all three of them. Currently we are scheduled for twenty-four parades and twenty-four competitions this year. If there are any questions you can ask your instructors."

I was amazed. Twenty-four parades. What is that all about? I couldn't wait to ask Eddie why they had scheduled so many of them. After all, I just wanted to compete. That was the reason why I had joined this organization. This parade idea just seemed a little ridiculous to me, and three in one day? They had to be kidding. That just seemed like a lot of unnecessary work to me. As soon as we got outside I grabbed Eddie and asked, "What is with all these parades we have scheduled? I thought we were a competition Drum Corps?"

Eddie just smiled and said, "We are, but we have to support ourselves some how. You see we get paid for each parade we do and that allows us to purchase equipment, uniforms, and pay for instructors. Why do you think we stressed taking care of the equipment so hard? It comes down to something very simple. The better we do on competitions, and parades, the more money we make as a Drum Corps and the more we can support ourselves."

I just absorbed all of this information. I couldn't believe what I was hearing. I was numb at first. My only response was, "So what I am hearing you say Eddie is that we are basically a professional organization that gets paid for the work we do.

And the better we do the more we get paid." That realization surprised me. Not only had I completed something that I really wanted to, I could be considered a professional at it. And that fact made me a little nervous. I wasn't ready to be considered that yet. And I knew it.

Eddie's response was accompanied by a smile, "Exactly."

Then I had to ask:" You said that the some of the money is used to pay for instructors. Do you get paid for doing this?"

Again Eddie just smiled at me and said: " No, I don't get paid for doing this. I just enjoy being part of the drum corps."

And again he had left me completely dumbfounded with his response. To think that this man, the instructor of a winning color guard for the past four years, competed against other instructors who get paid, and he did it for free just threw me completely. I found myself having a newfound respect for him after that. All the way home I kept thinking about that conversation with Eddie. I wondered if it was going to be worth it for me. After all I was the guy who had always taken the easy way out of everything. And this was beginning to sound an awful lot like work to me. *Three parades in one day.* I still couldn't believe it. On the way home what Jack had said finally sunk in. But I decided that I would try it and see how it went. After all I felt very comfortable with these guys and really enjoyed being with them. We had fun together and we seemed to understand each other. And I had completely forgotten about the death of the infants or being invisible while I was with them.

I decided that this could be fun. At least I could rationalize it that way for now.

When I told Doug about it he laughed and said, "You guys have got to be nuts. Three parades in one day. No way possible for me."

And I started wondering if it was really possible for me to march in three parades in one day. This was going to be a real challenge. There was nothing I could do about it now. But I couldn't get it out of my mind. Really, *three parades in on day*. The thought of going from one parade to another just boggled my mind. How is that physically possible? How do these people keep doing this year after year? The only answer that I could come up with was that these people really had to love it. There just wasn't any other explanation for me. That had to be it. And do you know what? I agreed with them. I loved it also.

Parades

Before Memorial Day came, Eddie had informed us that we would all meet at the VFW hall and leave our vehicles in the parking lot. I was riding with him so it didn't bother me at all. It just meant that I had to rush over to his car after the parade. He then explained that we would get a ride to the beginning of the parade in Westfield. He said that the parade was only about four miles long and as soon as we were done we had to get right into the vehicles to go to Russell for a two-mile parade, which would then be followed by another one-mile parade in another town. Needless to say, I was still confused about these *three parades in one day* but I was determined that I was going to try it. After all, my brother was also doing it with me. And I had figured that if he could it then this might be the one thing that I could keep up with him on.

When we got to the beginning of the parade I was amazed. There in front of me were hundreds of people milling around. Some in Drum Corps uniforms, some in high School band uniforms, all visiting with each other and practicing. And everywhere you went there were snare drums practicing drum rolls. To me this was amazing. I couldn't believe the closeness of all of these people knowing that they all competed with each other. And yet here they were helping each other. It was exciting to watch. This was the real show, not the parade.

It was hot that day. The weatherman said it was going to top out at eighty-five degrees. For that time of the year that was hot. I just couldn't get that fact out of my mind. All I could think of was wearing this heavy black wool uniform in that heat.

And I wasn't looking forward to it at all. I continued looking around. I was looking for my brother, John. He had gotten there before us.

I finally found my older brother in the crowd. He was dressed in the uniform of our high school band. He was planning on marching with them for the first parade and joining us for the other two afterwards. He had left his drum corps uniform at the VFW hall. He just smiled at me and said: " Are you ready for this little brother?" I could only nod in response to his question.

Then I noticed a color guard practicing. I looked carefully and thought I recognized some of the members. Bobby, Dick, Gary, and Danny all came over to me at that time. I asked them, "Who is that Color Guard over there?"

Bobby responded, "They are the Liberty Drum Corps Color Guard and they are also from Westfield."

Now I understood why I recognized some of them. I had played little league baseball with some them. As I watched them I had to ask, "Is that their practice equipment they are working with?"

Dick just looked at me and asked, "What do you mean?"

I responded with, "Well those rifles look like they were purchased in a toy store. They look like a piece of lightwood with a gun barrel glued to the end and black tape on the rifle butt. Let's face it. They are not Springfield 1903's. And those flags have round knobs on the top of them, not spears or eagles. Besides that their flagpoles look like they are about half the size of ours."

Dick just looked at me and said, "What they are carrying is all that they are required to use for competition."

I just looked at him and asked, "You mean those aren't training rifles they are carrying?"

Bobby laughed, then joined the conversation by saying, "No they are not."

I couldn't hold myself back. I just had to ask, "What you are trying to tell me is that we do things the hard way and carry the more difficult equipment. We also teach our competitors, (that fact still bothered me) and we still win anyways."

Dick responded with, "That is what we do."

I just shook my head and said, "Boy, if they ever figure out what we do we are going to be in some serious trouble."

Dick again responded, "I agree, but until they figure it out we will just keep on winning." Then he walked away.

And I just stood there watching him as he walked away, absorbing what he had just said, and thought to myself, " They are talking about us working against a stacked deck, and we still win anyways." This really threw me. All I could think of was, " Can they possibly make it any more difficult for us?"

Slowly the color guard migrated together. We were all in uniform now and to me this was an impressive sight. You could tell we were all nervous. Our season was about to start. Our conversations were very short and had nothing to do with what we were about to do. Gary suddenly said, "The Oakland Raiders football team has the right idea. Their motto is" In search of excellence."

Bobby responded with, "Unfortunately, excellence is not good enough for us. For us it's perfection or nothing at all."

And again one of the brothers had thrown me all off. Perfection, I had to think about that one. I had to admit. To me it *almost* made sense. After all we carried the most difficult equipment you could ask for, and taught our competition. I figured that if we were going to continue our winning ways we had to strive for perfection. This was a scary thought for me. I was starting to understand something that a few months ago I would never have considered. What a strange feeling.

Then Robert came over to us with a very stern determined look on his face and told us to fall in. Suddenly, when I looked at the others I saw that same determined look on their faces.

The Drum Corps started to form up at the same time. Robert then walked up to each member of the color guard one at a time to see if his uniform and equipment were ready for the day. After he had checked out each person he asked them each the same question." Are you ready to take a walk?'

The experienced members responded with, "Let's walk."

Robert would then nod to them and go on to the next person. When he came to me he asked the same question. I was so nervous I could only nod. Robert smiled a little, nodded back, and moved on to the next person until he had checked out every member of the color guard. And had asked them all the same question.

Then the corps started with a drum roll and went immediately into a song. My nerves were now the size of elephants and I was surprised that my body was still inside the uniform. Then it happened. It was a loud roar from all of the drum corps in the area. It took me a few seconds to realize that the other drum corps were cheering for us.

When it did sink in I began to understand how much respect the organization had amongst its peers.

Then Robert gave us the command to step off and we did so with all of the pride we could muster. That parade went by like a blur for me. All I could remember was the cheering crowds and running to the cars to get to the next parade. When we got back to the cars Eddie told us to take our jackets off and put them into our garment bags for the trip to the next parade. I was relieved to get that jacket off. It was hot marching in that wool jacket. I then started taking my sweatshirt off, and Eddie stopped me by saying, " Leave that on. If you take it off now you'll never get it back on for the next parade."

So I left the sweatshirt on. It was extremely uncomfortable. The sweatshirt was soaked all the way through.

Once we got in to the cars I asked Eddie, " So where is the next parade?"

He just turned to me and said, "It is in Russell. It's a short parade, only about a mile long, with a ceremony immediately following. You guys will have to stand there at attention while the local VFW members give a talk."

That didn't seem like it was going to be too bad to me. So I just relaxed as much as I could for the rest of the ride to Russell.

Eddie was right. The parade itself was only a mile, and after doing the previous parade it was easy. What he didn't tell us was that the VFW members were going to talk for a good forty-five minutes while we all stood at attention. This was brutal. Especially in that heat. I was just standing there praying for them to complete their ceremonies.

Don't get me wrong I did understand why the ceremony was important to them. And I even understood why we were there.

But the sweat was just running down my face and I couldn't do a thing about it. There was a slight breeze coming up now and that was a welcome relief. The wind would move the flag out of my face and begin to cool me down. Unfortunately when the breeze was over the flag was once again draped across part of my face and I could feel the beads of sweat starting to form on my face.

Out of the corner of my eyes I could see members of the drum corps fainting from the heat. They would collapse straight to the ground. Losing all control of their bodies. Through all of this Eddie and the other adults that traveled with the drum corps were busy administering smelling salts to the fallen members of the drum corps to revive them. Then I remembered what Eddie had always told us. Namely, never lock both of you knees at the position of attention. Always unlock one of them and shift your weight from one leg to the other when you are standing for long periods of time. You know what it works. And if you do it right no one will ever notice it. I spent the total time standing shifting my weight from one leg to the other.

By the time the ceremony was over I was drenched in sweat. I found it difficult to move. When we got back to the cars I couldn't wait to get that jacket off and drink some nice cold water. In fact, I wanted about a gallon of it. Originally, I thought I wanted a cold soft drink. But Eddie told us earlier not to consume any until the day was over. His reasoning was the sugar would run through our system and slow us down. So ice water was the drink of the day and it felt great.

Once we got back on the road I only had one question for Eddie, " Why didn't you tell us that the ceremony was going to be that long?"

He just looked at me and said, " I didn't know."

I could accept that. The thought of him knowing, ahead of time, that we had to stand there, in that heat, for that long, would have bothered me quite a bit. I would have definitely lost a lot of respective him if he knew about it. For now I accepted his answer.

The next parade was in a town that was only a few miles away. According to Eddie we just had to march about a mile and it would be over. All I could think of was that there was no way it could be any harder than what we had just done.

This parade went quick. It was a good thing. I couldn't wait for it to be over.

After it was all over I felt great. We had preformed in *three parades in one day* and I loved it. The only thing I could think of now was my mother's famous words: " You can do whatever you put your mind to." To me I had done that. I had decided that I was going to complete these three parades and I did. I would never admit it to her but she was right. And it felt good to have accomplished this.

The other members of the color guard all felt the same. We celebrated by going to the nearest fast food restaurant. We were tired and completely drained physically, and yet we were excited. And we were not ready to calm down. We had just finished *three parades in one day* and we weren't afraid to let the world know it.

When Danny and I got out of the car we jumped as high we could in the air and gave each other a high five, while screaming at the top of our lungs. " We did it. We did it. We did three parades in one day." The other members of the color guard just looked at us like we were crazy, but we needed this as a release for the day. There was no holding it in. We had completed three parades in one day and it was finally over. And it felt good to have completed it with them. In my estimation we had started of that day as a group of individuals and completed that day as a color guard.

The following weekend we had a parade in a nearby city. When we got there a policeman came up to us and informed us that the previous weekend they had a race riot in the area where the parade was scheduled to end and we should be very careful in that area. He also added that he had heard of a group of people who were planning on disturbing the parade route as much as they could. This disturbance was meant as a reprisal for the previous weekend. He really didn't think that they would really do anything but found it necessary to warn us anyway.

None of this seemed to matter to myself and the other members of the color guard. Our only concern was doing a good job during the parade. Before we stepped off Robert once again came up to each member and asked if he was ready to take a walk. This time I was able to answer like all of the others. This was to become a ritual that Robert would perform prior to stepping off for all of our activities including competitions. At the time I didn't know that but I would learn. All he was trying to do was calm us down and keep us focused on the job at hand.

The parade went well. The crowds were receptive and appreciative of the performance that the Drum Corps was providing. When we got near the end of the parade a policeman on a motorcycle came up to Robert and said that there were a group of people trying to disturb the flow of the parade by blocking off the route about a quarter of a mile before the scheduled end of the route. He told Robert that he would try to help out, but he had to monitor a lot of area, and he told us he would be there if he could when we got there.

Robert's response was, "Thank you" and the policeman just pulled away. His primary job that day was to keep the parade route as clear as possible throughout the full route.

He would travel up and down both sides of the parade route keeping the route clear of obstructions.

When we got to the location the policeman was talking about I could see that the crowd had completely enclosed the parade route and were standing about eight people deep in our path.

Robert had the color guard mark time with the music. He went and spoke to Bill, the Drum Major of the Corps.

He then came back and gave a speech, "Remember, you are members of the Whip City Drum Corps color guard. We go around no one, and we always finish what we start."

He then stepped to the right side of the color guard and gave a command that sent chills up and down my spine because I knew what it meant. The command was, "Parade manual trail arms."

To me it meant that I took the American flag out of it flag holder, pulled the flag up against the pole and held everything up against my right shoulder. For the other flags it meant something else. They would take the flags out of the flag holder, gather the flag into their right hand and place the end of the flag pole under their right shoulder while holding the flag pole straight out. The effect was that the bronze spears were about six feet in front of the color guard with the flagpoles looking like jousting lances from the Middle Ages. It was an intimidating sight. To see those bronze spears glimmering with the sun's reflection sitting six feet out in front of you just made you feel uncomfortable.

Robert then gave the command to step off. He immediately gave another command. It was, "To the right oblique march." As soon as he did this I knew what he was up to.

He was going to sweep the street from one side of the road to the other with those bronze spears to clear the parade route. I couldn't believe it. All of sudden I was feeling very uncomfortable. All I could think of was, " What is he going to do if they don't move?"

On this command the color guard all moved on a forty-five degree angle. He then ordered them, "To the left oblique march"

On this command we came to the center of the road again. His next command was once again, "To the left oblique march" and again we moved to the left on a forty-five degree angle.

He would continue this until they had completely swept from one side of the road to the other. And then he started back again. When we went by the crowd the first time I could tell that it was beginning to thin out. When we came back the second time, it was clear.

Robert then commanded us to mark time with the music. To myself I gave a sigh of relief. For the life of me I couldn't think of anything Robert could have done if they were still there. Then the only option would have been to go straight into the crowd. I had to think about that one. I seriously did not believe that he would have done that. But at least we didn't have to worry about it now. The bluff had worked. The parade route was clear.

He then gave the command to put our flags back into their flag holders. I silently gave a sigh of relief. I couldn't believe that we had just done that. Then the drum corps started up in song. The name of the song was the "Entrance of the Gladiators." It is also known as the Circus song.

The crowd, who had just recently blocked our way, was cheering like I had never heard before. We stepped off, and we did so with renewed pride. That song from then on was the color guard's song, and we stepped a little prouder to it whenever the drum corps played it. When we reached the end of the parade route the other drum corps were there and the applause we received was deafening. They had all seen what had happened and they were appreciative of it.

The policeman on the motorcycle came up to Robert after the parade and said, "I have never seen anything like that before. You guys don't fool around. All of the other drum corps just ended the march there, but not you guys. You guys are great."

Robert's response was short and to the point. "Thank you." And he walked away to get undressed.

From that point on everyone in the color guard completely trusted Robert. We knew that what ever he called for a command, we would follow it, without question. Our confidence in him, as our leader, was something that we would never question, and we trusted his judgment completely.

The next parade was scheduled to be six miles long. Eddie was concerned that the temperature, which was going to about ninety-five degrees with a humidity level of about eighty five percent, might bother us.

The color guard wasn't concerned; after all we had just completed parades of ten miles and eight miles. A six-mile parade was now a cakewalk for us.

When it came time for us to step off, Robert came to each person and asked if they were ready to take a walk, and we all responded appropriately.

As usual he stood in front and gave his usual speech, "Remember you are the Whip City Color Guard, you go around no one, and you always finish what you start." And then we stepped off to start our part of the parade.

I only remembered stepping off and ending that parade. The rest of it didn't even exist as far as I was concerned. It was a blank space of time that I could not account for. When Robert gave the command to fall out I felt weak, my knees were buckling, and I was having a hard time standing straight up, so I leaned up against my flag for support. I suddenly felt drained, and I didn't know why.

Eddie came running up to the color guard and starting yelling, "What is wrong with you guys? Didn't you know that Bill, the Drum Major, had stopped the Corps three times in the shade to give them a place to cool off? Why did you keep going? You realize don't you that you never stopped for the whole parade and the drum corps is about twenty minutes behind you?"

Eddie turned to me and said: " Mike, are you alright? You look like your going to pass out. Get in the shade quickly and take off that jacket."

I didn't hesitate to do what he said, and when I got to the shade he handed me a bottle of water and said: " Give me your flag. Sit down and drink this."

He wasn't going to get any arguments from me on any of those suggestions. You cannot even imagine how much cooler I felt once that jacket was off, and that cool refreshing bottle of water started reviving me almost immediately.

Each one of the members of the Color guard could only look at each other with confused looks.

Finally, Robert asked, "This is the end of the parade isn't it?'

Eddie just looked at him and said, "Yes, it is. Were you guys in some kind of trance?"

And then it hit us all. We were in a trance. We had completed the whole parade in a complete trance, and the last thing we wanted was to be reminded of it. Namely because we were all uncomfortable about not remember the whole parade. And the idea that we did it while in a trance just meant that we had no conscious control over what we were doing. And that thought bothered us. Who knows maybe it was a good thing. If it was really a meditation we could accept it. But if it was anything else we did not want to hear about it. We just all hoped that it was indeed some form of meditation for us. At that moment all we wanted was water, about a gallon apiece. Eddie then started giving us each water and had the rest of us all move into a shaded area while we waited for the Drum corps to arrive.

When the corps got their Bill, the Drum major, and my brother, John, came over. They both wanted to know if everyone was okay. My brother just asked, "Are you alright little brother?"

I knew he would be concerned. He was like that. But I also knew that he would never understand what we just went through.

My response was, "I am fine. I only need about a gallon of water right now." When I finally got to take off my sweatshirt that day I was surprised. It felt like I was pealing off my skin. It took me forever to do it. And it was heavy with sweat. I turned to Danny and said," Danny, come here a minute and hold one end of this sweatshirt."

He came over and held one end of the sweatshirt while I held the other end and started to twist it. He then commented, " I don't believe how much sweat is coming out of this thing. Do you really sweat that much?"

He was right. The sweat was just pouring out of the shirt. My only comment was," Obviously, I sweat that much." And we both laughed along with the other members of the color guard who had been watching during that incident.

From that point on the color guard had a tendency to perform in a trance state and, it didn't matter if it was a parade or a competition. We approached all of it the same. Everything we did from then on was purely reactive. We knew all of the moves, we completely trusted our leader, and we understood what was expected of us.

We had another parade scheduled the next week. The site of the march was only a few miles from our hometown so the travel time was short. As we were marking time before the start of the parade I noticed something out of the corner of my eye. It was a cameraman kneeling down in front of the left side of the color guard. He was getting ready to take a picture as we stepped off.

Just then a man came up to him with a drum corps jacket on, I didn't recognize the name of the drum corps only because I didn't know any of them at the time, and said to him, " I wouldn't stay there if I were you."

The cameraman just stared at him blankly and said:" Why not?"

The other drum corps person just looked at him and said: " Do you remember the story of the color guard that cleared a crowd recently?"

The other man said, " Yes, everyone has heard that story."

The drum corps person responded with," Well, that's them. And if a crowd is not going to stop them, how do you think they are going to feel about one cameraman?"

The cameraman just looked at him with a blank look on his face and said, " Oh." And moved slowly to the side of the road.

After seeing this I just smiled to myself. It appeared we had a reputation. What do you know? We had become famous.

The rest of that parade was uneventful. We went into our trance at the beginning and came out of it at the end. It was becoming a routine for us now.

Often times the parades that we marched in were quite a distance from Westfield. The ride there was usually very quiet. The way back could become a little rowdy. We would do extreme things to release our emotions. On one occasion we actually tied all of our sweatshirts to a rope and, with both cars driving side by side on route 91, ran the rope, with the shirts on it, between both cars. In essence we had created our own traveling clothesline

The color guard usually rode with Eddie and Bill. Billy, Gary, Danny, and myself were all riding in Eddie's car on one of these trips home one day when Bill's car pulled up along side.

Eddie immediately wanted to know, "What are these guys up to now?"

And there in the car beside us were five naked butts hanging out of the windows at us. Everyone just laughed. I just looked at them and said, "At least now we know who the biggest asshole is in that car."

Danny immediately asked, "And who would that be?"

My response was quick, "Why one of you brothers of course."

And we all laughed again. Then Gary responded with, "You guys, you do know that since they all just shot us a moon we have to respond."

We all agreed, and Eddie sped up so we could return the favor to the other vehicle. This action continued all the way home that night. It was fun. We laughed all the way home that night.

On another trip back from a parade one night we all stopped at a rest area on the way home. The people in the other car were taking an unusual amount of time getting out of the rest area, and Eddie was trying to rush them out.

He was concerned because we had an early departure planned for the next day and we were all planning on staying over his house that night, we couldn't leave until all of us went to Eddie's church for Sunday mass. After what seemed like an unusually long time both cars finally left the rest area. About three miles down the road the other car pulled along side of Eddie's. He just said, "Now what?"

When one of these cars pulled up beside you it always made you wonder what was going on. Then from nowhere there was a loud *splat,* against the side of the car, then another, and another. Then something hit Eddie's windshield and splattered all over it. It was water. Eddie had to turn on the windshield wipers to see while he was driving. Then one came into the window, hitting Danny in the shoulder and splattering all over everyone. Eddie was the first to speak, " What are those? Water balloons?"

Gary just chuckled, holding the remnants of the one that had hit Danny and said, "No, they are condoms filled with water."

Everyone just laughed. Eddie just shook his head and said, "That is why they took so long in the rest room. They were emptying the condom machine in there and filling them with water."

No one thought too much more of the incident at the time. We just went on to Eddie's house. It turns out that Eddie lived right next to the church so for expediency we parked the cars in the church parking lot for the night. When we got up the next morning we found out that Eddie was giving a talk during the church services that day. We were all right with that. We had all heard Eddie speak before.

The ceremony went well. Eddie gave a great talk about the bible. And he had done a good job of it.

When the services were over we all met Eddie outside. It turns out that he was the last one to leave the church that day. He had stayed behind for a few minutes to assist the priest in cleaning up the church. When we all went to the cars Eddie's face turned beet red.

There, right in front of the church, was his car with condoms stuck to the windshield and the radio antenna. He immediately ran to his car and started removing them as quickly as he could. Needless to say it was a very quiet ride to our activity that day and we all had to promise that we would never do that again.

Every time I got home Doug was there to ask how things went that day. He loved the story about the clearing of the crowd and the cameraman. He was amazed that we were being remembered that way.

I didn't tell him about all of us going in a trance. I wasn't sure that he would understand it. After all that was special to us. And we were not ready to share it with anyone. It still surprised me that anyone could continuously operate that way with any success.

Competitions

In between the parades the competition season started. The first one the Drum Corps attended was at a school in northern Connecticut. The color guard prepared for it the same way we did for all of our parades. We checked all of our equipment, polished shoes, and cleaned the brass on the flag spears prior to getting dressed. After that we unrolled and prepped the flags for the day. Once we got dressed, we knew that the time was near for us to find out what kind of color guard we were going to be that year. I could feel the anxiety inside of me building as we approached the competition field. All I could think of was that I didn't have to worry about locking my knees today. I only had to stop them from shaking and I would be all right.

Once we were formed up and were ready to step off Robert came around again to each man and asked if they were ready to take a walk. By now we were all able to respond to that question. At that point I remember sliding into the normal trance that we entered into for parades. It was a good thing, for when we stepped off the roar of the crowd was so loud that we couldn't hear any of Robert's commands. Instead everything became reactive. We all knew what was coming and when. So whenever Robert moved his head we new what the command was going to be and we just did it. As he moved his head from side to side we came closer and closer to our first competition. He called a right flank movement and followed it with a column left. When he called us to mark time I knew the time of the first competition was getting close. Then he called the commands of halt and left face. Here we stopped at the position of attention and waited for the judge to come over and take us through our presentation.

Once the judge came over to inspect the color guard everything moved very slowly. We started off by completing a present arms command. That is were all of the flags are brought down to a forty-five degree angle while the riflemen go to their present arms position. The judge then inspects each person in this position. Once he is satisfied he tells the color guard sergeant to go back to the right shoulder position. At this point he looks over each individual to ensure that they have preformed their commands correctly. It felt like it took him forever to look over each man and inspect the position of his respective equipment. It appeared to me that he was trying to find something wrong. He would stop at each one of us and look over our position in complete detail. When Robert gave the final salute it finally ended. I was glad to have it over.

When we finally got off the stand Eddie came over to us and told Robert to march us to the cars. At first I was concerned I thought that something had gone wrong. I found out later that Eddie like to keep everything to himself until no one else was around.

Once we were near the cars Eddie told Robert to stop the guard and asked him how it went. Robert then said, "Good, real good. Only, Mike's feet weren't at a forty- five degree angle, and Danny's spear was not straight."

Eddie's response was simple, "Guess what we are working on Thursday?"

We all new what was in store for us at the next practice. And we were going to do it *until we couldn't do it wrong*. At that moment I was trying to be cavalier about the whole thing. I kept telling everyone: " We'll do better the next time." All the while, thinking that I had just caused them to loose their first competition. I had let them down. And that was something that I was not happy about.

The last thing I wanted to do was let these guys down. To know that I would be the cause of them losing really bothered me. And yet I knew that I could do nothing about it.

Once we were done competing the equipment was put away. It was at this time that Danny asked me if I wanted to go watch some of our competition. Dick quickly spoke up, "We don't do that."

I just looked at him and said, "What do you mean we don't watch our competition?"

Bobby answered for him by saying, "We don't watch them because we don't compete against them. We only compete with ourselves."

Now this completely dumbfounded me. I really didn't know how to respond to this one. So I waited until after Bobby and Dick both left the area and asked Eddie what he meant. Eddie's response left me in amazement. He said, "It is simple. If you are running in a race and you keep looking back to see where you're nearest opponent is you fall behind. In fact more often than not you end up losing because you're only concerned with what your opponent is doing and you forget about what you are doing."

My only response was to myself. "Hmmm, Let me get this right. Do things the most difficult way possible, teach your competition, and only be concerned about what you're doing. Boy if this works it *is* amazing. "

And at the end of the day it did work. We had come in first place. We had won our first competition together. I was delirious with excitement. I couldn't believe how good it felt to be the part of the best color guard on the field that day. I had gotten a reprieve. I did not cause us to loose our first competition. And the relief of that moment was overwhelming.

Danny and I celebrated until we left that night for home. We couldn't control ourselves. We were just happy that we didn't let the others down after all.

All my life I had been told that in activity it is only important that you participate. Well if you go into it with that attitude there is only one thing you become. A participant. But if you are willing to do the work required, and learn more than anyone else on the subject, you can win. And there is no feeling so exhilarating as know that you are the best at something for that day. It is an addictive feeling. You just want to do it over, and over again. And we were ready to experience again.

The next couple of competitions had the same results. I couldn't believe that this philosophy really worked. But the proof was right in front of me.

Danny and I were walking around the area after competing one day and got quite a surprise. It seemed that wherever we went there was a group of young girls and guys following us. We were beginning to wonder about it. They were showing up everywhere we went. Danny finally decided to find out what it all about and asked them: " Are you guys following us?"

One of them responded quickly, "Yes we are."

The response spooked Danny and I for a second. I had to ask, " Why are you following us?"

The same person responded, " Because your part of the Whip City Color guard that's why."

Danny and I just looked at each other confused. He then asked them, " You know who we are?"

The same person responded again: " Of course. You are Danny. You carry a flag. You live in West Springfield, and you are a sophomore in high school. The other guy is Mike. He carries the American flag, lives in Westfield and is also a sophomore in high school."

Danny and I could only look at each other in amazement. They knew everything there was to know about us. Where we lived, as well as where we went to school. We were shocked. And then it hit Danny and I both. We both said, with a smile; " We are celebrities. We have groupies. Can you believe it?"

I was surprised at this to say the least. Everywhere we went from that point on we had someone following us. It became very interesting at times. If we wanted to get something to drink or eat they volunteered to get it for us. Often times they would bring us over to the members of their drum corps just so they could introduce us as their friends. We had people waiting on us. And whenever a color guard thought we could help them we ended up teaching them. It was a unique feeling for us. We were considered experts in our field. We loved it. We were the center of attention and we were completely enjoying it.

Then one day Danny and I got the bright idea of putting our newfound celebrity status to work for us. So we asked our groupies to help us get ready for our next competition. At first this worked great. One of them was polishing my shoes while another was cleaning the bronze spear for Danny's flag, and they were very conscientious about it. At every step of the process they would come and ask us if they were doing it right. We were really enjoying this newfound celebrity status.

Then Eddie showed up. The first words out of his mouth were," You girls have to leave here now. I want to talk to Danny and Mike."

Right about now both Danny and I expected to get chewed out for a long time. Instead Eddie surprised us. He just stood there for a second and said: " You can do whatever you want with your little groupies away from the color guard. But here you do your own work. You take care of the equipment. No one else is going to do it for you. You two have to remember something. With fame or notoriety comes a certain responsibility. You have to treat these people like you would like to be treated. I 'm absolutely certain that if someone had asked you to do their work for them you two would feel very used. Why would you ask someone to do it for you? Besides take a look around you. Haven't you noticed that the other members of the color guard also have people constantly following them and offering them all kinds of things? The difference is that they know, the other members of the color guard that this kind of fame comes with a certain amount of responsibility and they have accepted it. Are you ready to do the same?"

Eddie just walked away shaking his head.

Danny and I just looked at each other. We knew he was right. We knew that we had to start accepting some responsibility for our actions. We both just shrugged our shoulder and said: " It was fun while it lasted."

We were ashamed of what we had done. Taking advantage of someone was not something we wanted to be any part of. Eddie was right.

From that point on we always did our own work on the equipment. Don't get me wrong; we still enjoyed the celebrity status. We were just going to make sure that no ever did our work for us again. We knew that we were responsible for our own equipment and we were ready to accept that responsibility.

Once the competitions were over and the scores were being tallied the real fun of the day began. Normally there was about an hour to an hour and a half before any awards were given out. That's how long it took them to tally and recheck the scores before the announcements would begin. It was during this time that drum lines from the different drum corps would have their own competition. They would come on the field opposite their competitors and play to the middle of the field until they met face to face. It was here that they started demonstrating what they were capable of to each other. Once the demonstration was over they formed one drum line and proceeded to play together for the full length of the competition field. It was about this time that members of all of the drum corps would join in for a very large jam session. The music would range from classical to modern. It was amazing to watch how they could all work together.

Billy, Gary, Danny, and I loved to watch this. It was everyone letting off steam. They had put everything they had into the competition that day and they needed to release all of their nervous energy. To me this is what drum corps was all about, people working together to produce something exciting and beautiful

Danny and I were helping Eddie put the equipment away after one of these competitions when two young girls, in drum corps uniforms, came up and talked to Eddie. This didn't bother Danny or myself because drum corps people were always stopping by to speak to Eddie.

Eddie turned to us and said, "Mike and Danny come here a minute. These two young ladies want to know if you can help them with their rifle manual."

Danny and I just looked at each other and said, "Why not?"

After all, Eddie did make sure that we all knew rifle manual and we didn't mind sharing our knowledge. So we proceeded to teach the two young girls. It didn't take us long before we realized that it was not going to be easy. We just kept going over certain moves time and time again. No matter what we did they were not together. Then we remembered the counting that Eddie always had us do and we decided to try it with them. It worked. They were beginning to get the timing right. We were surprised to say the least. They weren't perfect but it was coming together.

Soon after we had started this activity, Bobby and Dick came up. They both just looked at what Danny and I were doing and smiled. It was Dick who broke the silence by saying, "It is about time you guys got the message."

I just looked at him and asked, "What do you mean?"

Bobby responded by saying, "It simple enough. It is about time that you two realized that Eddie is not teaching us just to be a color guard. He is teaching us how to teach." Once again Bobby and Dick had left me with something to think about. And again they had confused me. It was getting to the point that whenever they would say something I was getting surprised. I quickly decided to store every one of their comments until I was at home and try to sort out their meaning when I was alone. That was the only way I could deal with what they were saying. If I thought about it afterwards and put it in the right context it made sense to me. I was surprising myself. I had to admit that I was learning in spite of myself.

The next five competitions went the same way. The color guard was winning every time and we were beginning to get an ego about it.

Then one day, while on the stand, a large gust of wind came along as they were bringing our flags up to the right shoulder position. The wind had thrown me off so the flag missed the flag cup and I was standing there holding the flag by my right arm without any support from the flag cup. To make matters worse every time the wind gusted I felt my body move. And I just knew that that judge caught every one of those movements. The judge probably took one point off every time I moved. I could not wait to get off the stand. This time I just knew that I had caused the color guard to lose a competition.

When we finally got off the stand I was surprised to learn that Danny had also missed the flag cup and we were both moving with the wind while on stand. Needless to say, we did not win that competition. In fact we came in second during that competition. When the awards were given out silver medals were awarded to the second place color guard. Robert, Bobby, and Dick came over to us to give us our medals. Robert handed them to each member and said, "Take a good look at them. Now give them back to me."

The others and myself were confused, but we gave them back to him. He then turned to Bobby and said, "Explain it to them."

As he walked away, Bobby then told us, "The reason Robert took those medals back is that we do not accept second place in this color guard. He is going to give them to some deserving junior color guard. Before you say anything take a look at our drum major over there. He currently has over five hundred first place medals. He does not keep any medal under first place. Remember we only get concerned about coming in first."

With that he walked away. I just looked at the others and said, "Lesson learned the hard way as usual."

The others just smiled and nodded. After that experience we had learned a lot. The first and foremost lesson was that our ego couldn't write a check that our body could not cash. We had become complacent about our performances, expecting to win without working for it. We just thought that we could continue winning without staying focused on the job at hand. We found out differently. And secondly, we did not like **not** coming in first. From that moment on we did not loose another competition that year. We made sure of that. Needless to say the ride was very quiet on the way home that day. Eddie did break the silence with the following question; " Hey Mike and Danny what happened to your groupies after you guys came in second?"

Danny and I just looked at each other. We both seemed to realize at the same time that they were nowhere to be found when the announcement of us coming in second was made. Usually they were all around us when the awards were announced.

Then Eddie continued with his question, " Fame is a pretty fleeting thing isn't it? It probably feels like they are a pretty fickle group to you to. But you have to remember that they only want to be around winners, and today you lost. That just shows you how easy it is to be knocked off that pedestal"

We both just looked at each other. Danny spoke first, " You know what, he is right."

My response was simple, " Yeah, I know I just hate to admit it." We had learned a good lesson that day, a Lesson that we would not soon forget.

While we were cleaning up after one of the competitions I mentioned that I couldn't wait to tell my classmates about this whole drum corps experience. Eddie, Gary, Billy, and Danny were all there with me at the time and Eddie was the first to speak.

He just looked at me very calmly and said, " I wouldn't bother, besides, they would never understand it."

I was confused. I had to ask, "Why not?"

In my mind we were a well known and recognized drum corps. And we even had a strong following of people cheering us no matter where we went.

Eddie just looked at me again and said, "My niece is in one of your classes. Her whole world is wrapped up in trying to be accepted and being popular. You guys, don't fit in that mold and besides, they would never understand it."

I was confused. Eddie continued with the following questions. "Do you trust the members of the color guard?"

My response was, "Completely."

Eddie said, "They would never understand that. Do you feel comfortable being honest with the other members of the color guard? Are you guys respected by adults for what you do?"

My response to his both of his questions was, "Yes."

Eddie then continued, "The essence is that they are only concerned with their world and could never understand this one. It is not even worth saying anything to them."

It was about then that Billy chimed in, "Besides that they would never understand what it is like being cheered by hundreds of people every time we step off the line."

Then Danny spoke up with, "Besides that they would never understand what it is like being trained by Eddie."

At this point Eddie just said, "That will be enough out of you guys. Now get out of here and go have some fun."

As the four of us walked away I remembered Eddie's words about the two different worlds and it was making sense to me. That was a scary thought. He was teaching us something that I had never thought of. Again I was amazed.

About the middle of the summer my older brother and I got a phone call from Eddie. It turned out that one of the trumpet players, in the drum corps, had an accident while driving some friends home after school one day. He had died in the crash. It turned out that it was John's best friends in the Drum Corps and a previous individual trumpet Northeastern champion. The death of his friend bothered John a lot. He was crushed. John was not accustomed to letting his emotions out. I knew this. And yet I understood how he felt. I remembered how I felt after the death of the two six-month old infants and I couldn't even imagine the heartbreak of losing a friend that quickly. I knew that trying to talk to John would be a waste of time. He never let his emotions out. And this time I felt sorry for him because of that.

When the time came for the funeral John was asked to play taps at the ceremony. This was the first time I was concerned about my older brother. I wasn't sure how he was going to hold up against this task. You have to understand something; we never hung around with each other during drum corps. He had his drum corps friends and I had mine. This was one of John's closes friends.

As John played you could feel the tears in the music. After the ceremony I went over to John. Tears were sill coming down his check. I just asked, "Are you okay little brother?"

This time it did not mean that I was trying to get him angry. I was concerned. He never let his emotions out. And yet they were there in that song. He had found a way to express himself. And it was very moving. Even to me.

John just nodded. Then Eddie and the director of the Drum corps came up to them. Eddie was the first to speak, "That was beautiful," was all he could say to my brother.

The drum corps director just looked at John and said, "I have heard that song played a lot, but never like that."

John, for the first time, had let his feeling come through in his music. And with that he had reached everyone there that day. It was a very unusual for me to feel the music, but I did. And I had a newfound respect for my brother. He had found a way to let his emotions out about the event without the risk of exposing what was in his heart. It was beautiful.

State Championships

It was about the end of June when Eddie started talking to the color guard about the State championship competitions coming up. The first was the Connecticut State Championship scheduled to take place in July, and the second was Massachusetts State Championship in August. He then proceeded to explain to everyone that the only way to be eligible for the Northeastern States Championship was to win one of these two state championships. Otherwise you couldn't compete in the Northeastern States Competition.

About two weeks before the Connecticut State Championship, Eddie called for two practices a week. The color guard would practice on Tuesday and Thursday evenings. They were also closed practices, which meant that no one was allowed to visit those practices. To me it meant that no one could teach our competitors through that time. All through these practices the same message kept coming through. We are going to do these things *until we could not do it wrong*. That message was something that we were getting accustomed to. When the

MICHAEL WALSH

Connecticut State Championship came we felt good. When we got there we found out that there was one hundred and eight drum corps competing that day. I couldn't believe it. I had never seen that many drum corps in one place before. I had to know how many color guards we were competing against.

When I asked Eddie I couldn't believe the answer he gave me. "Somewhere around forty or fifty. It doesn't matter though, the only ones we are worried about are ourselves."

The number impressed me. The rest of Eddie's answer didn't surprise me at all. I was finally getting it.

Going on stand for this competition was just like all the other competitions we had taken part in, and we were ready. My knees no longer shook constantly while we were on the competition stand. I no longer got massive butterflies in my stomach before the competition. They were only controllable little ones now. The time we spent on the competition stand seemed shorter than some and longer than others. I was getting accustomed to being there. It was becoming comfortable for me.

Once we got off the competition stand Dick and Ray both went off to compete for the individual rifle competition. As they were leaving Eddie said, "You know the interesting part of that individual rifle competition is that no one in this color guard cares who wins as long as a member of this color guard comes in first and the other comes in second."

As it turned out the awards were not going to be given out until about 1:00 in the morning and the corps had a long ride home, with an early parade the next day. So it was decided that the majority of the drum corps would leave. A few, those who lived the closest would stay for the award ceremony and let the corps know the results the next day at the parade.

The next day everyone was anxious to find out how we had done. We couldn't wait for the people who had stayed behind for the awards to show up. Finally, they got there. Eddie went over to see them. He came back to the color guard and told Robert to form the guard up. H addressed us with the following: "You are now the Connecticut State Champs, and Dick is now the Connecticut State individual rifle Champ, with Ray coming in second place."

I was out of control with excitement. The others and myself were so happy that we just hugged each other and jumped up and down and screamed at the top of our lungs. Ray, who had come in second, to Dick, was just as happy as everyone else. He was ecstatic that Dick had come in first, and he second. I turned to Eddie and said; "I see what you meant about those guys now."

Eddie just smiled, and said, "All right, we have a parade to do, let's go to work." Robert got us ready to step off again, except now we were the Connecticut State Champions, and we marched with a new swagger because of it.

In the beginning of August the Massachusetts State Championship came along. The only difference was that Bobby and Ray competed for the individual honors this time. There were about thirty other color guards there for us to compete against, but by this time that didn't bother us. We were just going for it. As it turned out we won. It was starting to become commonplace for us. It was our comfort zone. We liked winning. And we were going to do everything we could to continue doing it.

Bobby also came in first in individual rifle, which meant that he and Dick would compete against each other at the Northeastern States Championship. It was an interesting scenario to say the least for two brothers to be competing against each representing two different state championships, but it happened.

When I informed Doug that we had won both state championships his only response was, "Even a blind monkey gets lucky sometimes."

My only response to this was, "I guess you're right." And we both just laughed about it together. He was playing our old game again, and I knew it. We had astonished him, and that fact felt good to me.

Northeastern Competition

After winning both Championships the color guard had a decision to make. We could go to the Northeastern competition representing only one state; we could not represent both of states. Eddie had gotten the color guard together after one of our practices and explained that fact to us. And it was time for us to make a decision as to which state we would represent. According to him it was only fair to let the other color guards know so they would have a chance to get ready for the competition.

It was Bobby who asked, "Who was our closest competition?"

Eddie explained that it was a color guard from Connecticut. Bobby's response was simple, "Well then why don't we go representing Massachusetts and allow them to compete from Connecticut?"

All of us in the color guard just looked at each other and nodded. By this time we had learned that Bobby was not going to pick the easy way out of anything. Eddie then said, "It's agreed then. I will let them know. This is going to make the other color guards in Massachusetts very angry but it is the right thing to do."

I didn't bother fighting this idea. I finally understood what this group was all about. It was simple. The better the competition, the better we performed, and for the first time it didn't bother me. I was accepting it. The challenge for perfection is what we were really all about and it had finally sunk into me.

When we started practicing for the Northeastern States Championship competition I was once again taken off guard.

It all started when Eddie handed us all a sheet of paper while saying, "The commands on this sheet are what you are going to be judged on during the competition for the Northeastern States Championship. Get to know them."

I looked at the sheet and commented, "Eddie did you make a mistake? This is the individual rifle sheet you used to judge us earlier this year."

Eddie just smiled and said, "There is no mistake. That is what you are going to be judged on as a color guard during this competition."

My mouth could only form the word, "Whoa."

The reason for my response was obvious, at least to me. On that sheet were the same moves that had we done as individuals for the rifle manual, and every one of them gave a judge multiple places to find something wrong with a full color guard performing them. This was more than a little intimidating. To me it was beginning to look like an impossible task. "How could anyone possibly do well having to compete this way?"

That was the only question that was going through my mind. All these moves, all these opportunities to make mistakes, all the different places a judge could find something wrong. These are the thoughts that I kept going over in my head. Then we started practicing. As usual we practiced until we couldn't do it wrong.

Again the counting was put into place. Every movement was timed to perfection. If Eddie didn't like the sound of it, or if it didn't sound together we just kept going until it was together. It was frustrating to practice like this at first. Then when the timing was coming together it felt great. All we wanted to do was continue working on it until we couldn't get it wrong. There goes that concept again.

For me it was working without question. As we got closer to the competition we all started getting more and more nervous about what we were about to do.

When we got to the competition it all hit home. This was the place where the best in the Northeast competed. There were no easy color guards to beat here. As the day went on the whole color guard started getting nervous. The first thing we had to do was escort the Corps onto the competition stand so they could compete musically. When they got off the stand we marched over to where the color guard stand was.

Here Eddie just looked us all over and said, "Well this is it. What you have worked all year for. Now go and show them what you can do."

Then Robert got out in front of the color guard, and before he could give a command Bobby asked, "Hey did you forget something?"

Robert smiled and came up each member and asked if he was ready to take a walk. One by one we all gave him the standard answer. One by one we all said let's walk. That finally meant that we were all ready.

Once we were in position the judge came over to Robert and said he could begin now. With that Robert gave the command to start the competition. The experience took about twenty minutes. Every movement of the guard was examined in detail by the judge. And this process continued for all twenty-one commands on that sheet. I thought we would never get off that stand. But finally it was over. All we could say was that we had tried our hardest.

Not even Robert had any idea how we had done.

Namely because all during the experience he could only give commands from out in front and hope that we were doing well behind him.

The judge never gave an indication of how it was going. He would just tell Robert which command to call next. Thankfully it was over.

At this time Bobby and Dick went off to the individual rifle stand. The Individual rifle stand was located across the competition field. We just watched as they walked away wondering if the two brothers could indeed be the Northeastern Individual Rifle Champions that day.

It was hours before they were ready to announce the awards. When they finally started the first thing they mentioned was that only the winner would be announced each category. This was completely different than the other competitions. At the other competitions they would announce all of the winners down to third place. But then again this was the Northeastern States Championships. If you won here you were the best in the Northeast. And that meant something.

The first awards given out were for the Drum Corps. I was concerned about this one because my brother, John, had been working hard for this one. And would you believe it our Drum corps won. They had beaten the best in the Northeast musically. That was an impressive thing to me. Especially since there were some very big named drum corps there that day. Then came the color guard announcement. A hush came over the crowd. "And the winner is Whip City."

The members of the color guard went crazy. We just screamed and jumped all over. We had done it. We were the best in the Northeast that year. It was an amazing feeling. And we liked it. Then we heard the individual rifle announcement. Another hush came over the crowd.

And the announcement went something like this, "We find ourselves in a peculiar situation. We are going to announce a first and second place award for this category only because of what happened is so unusual. In second place with and unheard of score of ninety seven, Richard Grover from Whip City, and in first place, with a score of ninety eight, which is completely unheard of, is someone we believe that he is related to, Robert Grover from the Whip City color guard."

The color guard couldn't believe it. They were all over the brothers congratulating them. Bobby and Dick were jumping around and screaming with excitement. It was the most emotion I had ever seen from either one of them. It was at this point that I realized how much coming in first and second meant to the two brothers.

It was about two weeks later when I was sitting on my front porch, that I finally took the time to absorb all that I had learned that summer. I was no longer a smart mouth young man who thought he know all of the answers. I was beginning to understand that there were more questions than there were answers.

I had seen and done some unusual things that year. I also realized that my mother might have been right after all. Those words of hers kept resounding through my head, " You can accomplish whatever you put your mind to doing." I found myself in a unique situation. I had to admit that she was right. I had found something that I wanted to do and it had worked out. I also decided at that time that I was not going to admit it to her. Instead it would become something for me to remember for the future. Besides I couldn't possibly tell my mother that she was right. After all that would be admitting that her mantra worked, and I wasn't about to do that. Instead, I was enjoying the learning that I had experienced. And I was going to keep that to myself for now.

I remembered people competing with sprained wrists, broken arms, and even some with walking casts on that year. The one person that really threw me was the individual that had to have their shoe cut off after every competition because their feet swelled up so much. This was a real eye opener for me. To love competing that much, that you would be willing to stand physical pain, was something that I was beginning to understand.

When Doug found out about the outcome of the Northeastern States Championship competition he could only say, "There goes that blind monkey again."

And once again we would both laugh about it. For we had amazed him so much that he couldn't think of anything else to say. It was that game of ours again. And I knew by his response that we had left him speechless.

PART THREE

Second year

The school year had once again started. This was something I was not looking forward to. But I went anyways. After all the idea of not going was something that I knew would not be accepted by my parents. This year was different somehow. I no longer felt out of place for not being one of the popular crowd.

Instead, after remembering what Eddie had said, I almost felt sorry for them. They just didn't quite get it. I was now part of a different world and it felt good to me. I was lucky. I had Robert and Billy in the class with me. And whenever one of the popular students would do something to get attention, I would just turn to one of them and ask, "Do I act like that at the competitions?"

The response I usually got was, "If you did we would get rid of you," and we would all just laugh.

It was during this time that things changed for us as a family. You see our father had been working days at the same job since he had gotten out of the Navy. He was a member of an assembly line in a manufacturing facility, and he was good at it.

He came home one day with some disturbing news. His job at the factory was going away, and he had to find something else to do. He did have a plan. Once he had calmed down our mother he came upstairs to John and I to talk about it. It turned out that there was a security position open at the company where he worked for a second shift person.

He went on to explain to us that it would mean that that he would work from 3pm in the afternoon to 11pm at night. I just looked at him when he said this and asked, " Why are you doing this?"

He looked at me very calmly and said, "So I can support you, your brothers and your mother. You'll understand this someday. For now what I need is to have you help your mother around here while I am at work. She is going to need a lot of help with your younger brothers."

John and I just looked at him and agreed that we would try to help out. Our father had been an important part of both John and my life to this point. He was always doing things with us. Granted our mother was better at baseball, and she could play board games better than him, but he always tried. And that was important to us. He always spent time with us. Now our younger brothers, Rick and Joe, were probably not going to have that experience, and at that point I started feeling bad for them and decided that I would try to fill in for dad in these situations.

Our brother Rick was pretty tall and thin for his age. He was five years younger than me and stood up to my shoulders at this point in his life. Where as our youngest brother, Joe, was just the opposite. He was stocky like us and a little shorter than people his age.

After a couple of months I started noticing a change in Rick. He was starting to get very defiant with me in particular. When

I thought about it, it made sense. He resented our father for not being there, and he definitely did not like me trying to take his place. Unfortunately I had no patience with this defiance, and I usually decided to hit him for it. Now that usually turned out to be a big mistake.

As soon as John found out he came after me for beating up our younger brother, and the confrontation with John always had the same ending. Me on the floor.

Needless to say I had to get even. So I went and beat up Rick again whenever John was not around. This way I didn't have to worry about having to deal with John getting even. Rick in turn would decide to beat up our youngest brother Joe. Now this always turned out to be a problem for Rick, because Joe could definitely defend himself and this usually resulted in Joe constantly getting the better of Rick. I felt sorry for Rick during this time he had nowhere to go with his anger. I will give him credit though. He found out that our mother would always defend him, and boy did we ever hear about that one from her. She was constantly chewing us out for picking on Rick. The only trouble was that, in my mind, as long as he had that attitude he deserved it.

Joe and I used to sit and talk together quite a bit now. On one of these occasions we were sitting on the front porch when we got into a discussion about what kind of person he wanted to be when he grew up. I just looked at him and said the following: " What you do is look at the people you admire the most. Look at what you like about them. Try to learn that from them, and try to put the kind of person you want to be together from that information."

His response just about blew me away. He just looked at me and said, " John is a very smart man, but he holds all of his emotions in. That is not good. You are not good in school, but you wear your emotions on your sleeve. Rick is very organized, almost as smart as John, and very arrogant. I think I want to be a mixture of all of you. I want to be smart in school like John, have fun like you do, and I want to be organized like Rick."

I just sat there in amazement. This child has got it all figured out. His response just threw me completely. To be that young and have such an understanding of his brothers really impressed me, and yet it made perfect sense to me. If I were going to emulate my brothers I would probably respond the same way. Now that doesn't mean that I would change. It does mean however that they each had qualities that I admired. After all I was still trying to learn what kind of a person I was. All I did know was that I was different from my brothers in many ways. I felt things differently than John. There is no way I could hold my emotions in like him. And I was not ever going to be running to our mother with all of my problems like Rick did. All I knew was that I was learning who I was through the drum corps experience and I was enjoying it.

There were many weeks during this period when I was excited about going to drum corps practices. I just wanted to be myself for a while. I needed it most of the time. Between drum corps and working at the grocery store I managed to spend a lot of time away from the house and I liked that. That way I didn't have to worry about taking care of my younger brothers. I knew that I was growing up more and more now. I was even accepting more and more responsibility now. I just wasn't ready to give up my old way of life without some kind of a fight. I was comfortable there and this new learning wasn't comfortable at all to me. I needed time alone to think about it.

My workday at the store usually started about 3pm in the afternoon. This gave me time to bring my schoolbooks home, change, and walk to work. John on the other hand started his workday right after school, which meant that he was there about an hour earlier than I was.

On one of these walks to work one day, I noticed someone watching me as I was coming towards him. I wasn't sure who it was at first. I kept walking. With each step the person was looking more and more like Larry, the individual from our experiences at the dyke. As I continued walking it became clear to me that it was him. There were all kinds of thoughts running through my head. The first one was, maybe he didn't notice me. Then it became clear that he was staring straight at me. The second thought was, if I cross the street maybe I can avoid any contact with him. Again it became clear to me that he was still staring at me, and the outcome of trying to hide from him would not work out well at all. So I just continued walking.

As I came closer and closer my nerves starting jumping all over the place, I felt like my heart was trying to jump out of my chest. When I came about ten feet from him he stepped right in front of me. I kept walking; I was to scared to do anything else. I starting envisioning myself getting to work with cuts and bruises all of my face. As I came up to him he stepped up to me and stared at me eye to eye. This action made me stop walking. I couldn't say a word. I just stood there.

Larry then spoke," I just wanted you to know that we haven't forgot about that promise that we made you."

I knew what he was talking about. I hadn't forgotten his threat. My heart starting beating a little faster.

He continued by saying, " The thing of it is that your brother John told us that if we hurt you we would have to deal with him. Now this didn't bother us at first until we watched him unload the meat truck last week. So we have decided to wait until he is not around to settle things with you and Doug."

And with that he stepped aside and walked away. The only thing I could do was let out a sigh of relief, and right away I wanted to get to work and thank my older brother. For the life of me I couldn't understand how he knew about the threat, and at this point I didn't care. All the way to work that day I kept asking myself that same question. How did John know? I knew I didn't say anything to him. Who did?

When I finally got to the store John was already unloading the meat truck. I walked up to him and told him what Larry had said to me. I ended the story with my nagging question, " How did you even know about that threat from them?"

John just looked at me and said: " Doug had told me about it. And before you say anything, that's how older brothers protect their family."

And he just continued unloading the truck. I just stood there. I couldn't believe that my older brother was showing affection. And once again he confused me. And once again I had gained another level of respect for him. I remembered him being able to express his emotions with his trumpet and how he had impressed me with it. Now he impressed me again. And again I was learning. This time the learning was from my older brother.

During one of the fall practices Eddie let everyone know that Robert was leaving the color guard to play baseball in the spring. This was no surprise. He was quite good, and he had played for the varsity team at our high school. We were disappointed. He was our leader. The only problem was that no one knew who was going to take over for him as the color guard sergeant. The answer came the following week of practice. It was going to be Bobby, and Gary was moving to right end as a rifleman.

Fortunately, there were two new members of the guard this fall that had to learn what it meant to practice until you cannot get something wrong. Again we were planning on having a ten-man color guard for the upcoming season. One of the new members was taller than I was and he was assigned to carry the American flag. This left me marching as a rifleman that year. And that was a welcome relief. No more wind to deal with.

We practiced all winter with just one thing in mind. We wanted to repeat our winning ways from the previous year.

It didn't take Bobby long to get acclimated to being out in front. He was a natural at it. It did take the new people a little time to accept the concept that perfection is what was expected of them.

All during the winter Doug would come over with messages from the Liberty Drum Corps color guard. It turns out that he had a couple of classes with three of their members. The messages were always the same. They kept telling Doug to let me know that they were going to win the Massachusetts. State Championship this year and that Whip City didn't have a chance because, according to them, they had a perfect group this year. My response was always the same. I would just look at Doug and say, "Good for them."

Doug would just laugh the whole conversation off and say, "Like they have a chance against you guys. But if you don't win I will never hear the end of it."

I just looked at him and said, " The Massachusetts State is a long ways off. A lot can happen between now and then. But if they are going to beat us they had better bring their best day to the competition."

When springtime finally came I was happy. I knew that the competition season was going to be starting soon. I was also happy that school was almost over for that year. My opinion of it hadn't changed, and I had once again proven that my theory of only passing the exams worked. I was being promoted to the next grade level. That was a surprise to me, but I knew better than to complain about it at this point.

Once the color guard started practicing outside everyone got excited, even the new members. They were however surprised when other color guards came to the practices to watch and take lessons. Billy and I just laughed at this and explained to concept to them. You could tell by the look on their faces that they were confused. I just looked at them and said, "I was just as confused as you are right now. The concept of teaching our competitors also bothered me at first, until I realized how it drove us to improve."

They still looked confused. I just walked away smiling because I knew how they felt. I also knew that they would understand it in time.

Then the season started. At the first parade I realized that these new people were going to do just fine. They also went into the trance while marching like the rest of us

They also enjoyed doing the best job they possibly could while they were in uniform. And now, as a rifleman, I got to experience a new sense of pride. Whenever we marched in a parade the riflemen always put on a little display during the parade. There is truly no explaining how good it felt to spin chrome-plated rifles into the air, catch them at the correct location, and have the crowd react to it. It was a lot of work but the reception the crowd gave us was worth it.

After each activity our new members were just like the rest of the color guard, ready to let loose with all of their emotions.

Their screaming was reminiscent of Danny and I celebrating after the three parades in one day. I recognized it and totally understood it. The rest of us were seasoned veterans now. It was commonplace for us. It was what we did.

The first competition came quickly that year. The more experienced members of the color guard, including me, were nervous about the new members. We didn't have the confidence we needed in their abilities yet. We didn't know how they would react to the extreme pressures that were about to come to them. That concern all came to a head when we went onto the competition field for the first time that year. As it turned out the new members did just fine. They went right into the usual trance like the rest of us. In fact the Whip city color guard came in first that day.

The next competition was going to be the real test. After all doing something once is fairly easy; being able to do it repeatedly is another issue all together. So, like all of the other experienced members of the color guard, I just waited to see what would happen with the next competition. As it turned out we won again. I was beginning to feel comfortable with the new members, but it was still going to take a couple of more competitions before I was completely ready to have the confidence I needed in them.

As the weeks went on we continued to win, and that impressed me. I was almost certain that we now had a Championship Color guard this year. Of course I would never admit it out loud. I also would never tell the new members that my confidence in them was growing. To me they still had to show what they were made of by having a consistent performance all season long.

While we were waiting for awards during one of the competitions something interesting happened.

The new members of the color guard were hanging around with Billy, Gary, Danny, and myself, after all we were experienced members of the guard now, when a line of snare drummers appeared on the competition field.

This didn't bother the others and myself because we had seen it before. The new members, however, where surprised at this. They couldn't believe how good they were. Gary then proceeded to explain to them that the drum line they were watching was made up of people from four different drum corps. Then he explained that the young drummer on the end was the instructor for all of them. The new members just looked at him with a confused look on their faces. Gary then explained that even though he was the youngest one out there, it didn't matter, because drum corps only recognize talent. And that young man had it.

The new members also found out what it was like having groupies. Needless to say Danny and I spoke to them about this. We both still remembered the hard lessons we had learned the year earlier. We were going to make sure that no one else in the color guard had to learn them the hard way like we did.

Even Doug was surprised with the Color Guard's winning record that year. In fact his comment was, "Maybe I don't have to worry about those guys from Liberty drum corps bragging."

As the Connecticut State Championship competition approached I was getting nervous. After all we had not lost a single competition all year up to that point.

Needless to say Eddie was also concerned.

On the day of the competition he got the color guard together and said, "Remember, you have won every competition you entered this year. Unfortunately, none of them mean as much as this one. If you win this one you have the right to compete in the Northeastern Championship. So let's go get it."

That was all it took. We won. And boy were we excited. The screaming and jumping went on and on. We had done it again. And this time with new people. It felt great.

By the time the Massachusetts State championship had rolled around we had not lost a single competition that year, and that thought kept bothering us. All we wanted to do was continue winning. We didn't care who was there to compete. All we knew was that we where once again striving for perfection.

Liberty Drum Corps was there that day. They competed against us along with about thirty other drum corps. All during that day, whenever we saw a member of their color guard they all had the same thing to say:" You guys are loosing today."

That is all they would say to us.

Our response was always the same: " Let's see what happens."

It is not that we were trying to be arrogant. Instead a lot of color guards had given us that message in the past and all of them had ended up losing to us. So as far as we were concerned this was an idle threat until they performed on stand. If they performed well enough to win we would be happy for them. Of course if we lost to them it would only mean that we would work even harder for the next competition to ensure that it would not happen again.

Unfortunately for Liberty Drum Corps, they lost to the Whip City Drum Corps color guard that day. We had once again managed to win the Massachusetts State Championship title. I could not wait to get home and let Doug know.

When he found out Doug was dancing around and saying, "I can't wait to see those guys in school next year."

Again the color guard had a choice to make. We had won both state championships and had to decide which state we were going to represent.

The choice was made the same way as the previous year. We simply asked, "Who was our closest competition? And we let them go."

The new members were a little confused by this logic but it was starting to make more sense to them little by little. Again we went to the Northeastern championship as the Massachusetts State Champions. And the color guard that came in second in Connecticut represented that state.

The Northeastern States Championship was in the state of New York that year. The drum Corps had to leave about six in the morning to get there in time for registration. We made it with time to spare. The new members of the guard were amazed at who was there that day. The others and myself had to keep reminding them of the fact that they were competitors that day, not spectators. They were fighting this concept. You could see it in them. This definitely gave me cause for concern. Eventually you could see it start to wear off of them and the fact that we were there to compete was starting to sink in.

When the time came they remembered. I also remembered something. How nerve racking this competition can be. I knew I was ready for it, but I wasn't sure how the new members were going to feel being scrutinized by that judge for twenty-one commands. All I knew was that there was nothing I could do about it now. They were just going to have to do their best. And hopefully that would be good enough. Again the experience took about twenty minutes, and again the results were the same. We had won another Northeastern States Championship title. Everyone was excited. Again we were there with the yelling and screaming. This celebration lasted for a good five minutes with all of us hugging each other constantly.

I felt good about that year. We had gone undefeated. I finally felt like I had contributed in making up for that one competition we had lost the previous year.

New York

As a surprise Eddie and Bill, the drum major, said they would take the color guard to New York City for an overnight trip because we did so well that year. My parents just looked at Eddie when they found out and asked, " Are you sure you want to take ten teenagers to New York City?"

Eddie just said, "They will be fine. They deserve it after the year they had."

So the plans were made for the color guard to go to New York City on a Saturday and to return on a Sunday. All the way their Eddie tried to prepare the members of the color guard. He kept warning us not to act like country bumpkins in the big city.

It was daylight when we got there. Once we got into our rooms and got settled we only wanted to do one thing. Go look this town over.

Eddie finally got us together about seven in the evening and said, "Bill and I are going for a good meal. If you guys want to you can join us. Otherwise, you can go look over the city."

To the rest us, that decision was a no brainer. We all decided to look over the city. Before we left Eddie told us, "Stay together all the time. Bobby and Dick you are in charge. Keep them all in one piece."

When we got outside it was dark, and we could not believe what they were looking at. There we were in the middle of Time Square on a Saturday night in New York City, with all of its neon lights aglow. We all just stood there with our mouths hanging open. People were everywhere. They were walking all over the street. It was a tremendous crowd.

About every third person was walking into a member of the color guard while we were standing there. This went on for about two minutes before Bobby said, "We better pick a direction to go in quick before we get rundown by these pedestrians. Let's go this way."

So we all went towards Time Square itself. Our mouths were still hanging open from seeing it for the first time. As we walked down the street, Danny spotted a restaurant. He suddenly remembered that he was hungry. He called out to the others and said, "Hey guys, let's get some food here."

We all agreed and went inside. It was basically a dinner in Time Square. The only open seats were at the counter so all ten of us sat down there. When the waitress came over I couldn't believe her attitude.

All she said was, "What do you want?"

We all just looked at each other and ordered cheeseburgers, fries, and a coke. When the food came she basically threw it in front of each one of us. As she was doing this she said, "Here is your check. The tip is already added into it. You can pay for it on the way out."

She then walked away never to be seen again.

After we ate our meal we were surprised when we looked at our bills. We were not impressed with our food, but it was edible, so we ate it. It was Gary who spoke first. After we had finished eating he looked at his check and said, "Eight dollars. For a cheeseburger, fries, and a coke. Do you know how many days I could eat at a fast food place with eight dollars?"

Bobby just looked at him, frustrated with his brother's comment, and said, "Let's just pay our bills and get out of here."

When we got outside Danny had to speak up, "Eddie had warned us that New Yorkers could be rude. But that waitress was the rudest person I have ever met."

As we continued to walk all over Time Square we were getting tired of the crowd of pedestrians we had to constantly maneuver around. So we decided so see what the side streets of New York had to offer. To our surprise it was nothing but nude shows and bars. Danny and I thought it would be interesting to try to get into the nude shows. Outside of each location was a bouncer and his job was to keep underage people like Danny and myself from getting into the establishment, and sure enough they did. With a curt tone they would just tell us, "Get out of here."

And Danny and I would walk away ready to try the next one. All this activity did separate us from the rest of the color guard, but that didn't bother us, as long as the others were still in our sight we felt comfortable.

After about the fifth time of being told to get lost someone spoke to us, "Hey are you guys looking for some fun?"

Danny said, "Sure. What have you got in mind?"

The man, who was about our height with a light brown jacket and a Yankees ball cap on, then said, "Come with me, I will show you where you can have a good time."

He then proceeded to walk down an alley. We followed him. The man then stopped suddenly and, while placing his right hand into his jacket pocket, said, "Alright, I have a knife in my pocket. Now give me all of your money."

Danny and I just looked at each other with a dumbfounded look. He had taken us completely by surprise. We were both suddenly very scared. When I looked at Danny I saw panic written all over his face. We were in a state of shock. This was the last thing we expected. The man spoke again and said; "Now look, there is only two of you, and I know how to use this knife. Now give me all of your money."

Then a voice was heard from behind the man. It was Bobby and he said, "I think you better count again."

Suddenly, I was relieved. Talk about the Calvary arriving in the niche of time. This was definitely on of those occasions. It felt good to know that someone was there to back us up.

The man turned his head slowly to see the other eight members of the color guard standing all around him.

He backed up a little and said, "I'm not looking for any trouble here. I am just trying to make a living. If it is alright with you guys I'll just leave now."

Bobby just looked at him and said, "Go on. Get out of here."

It took the man no time to get out of the alley. Bobby was very upset. He just glared at Danny and myself and said, "Can't leave you two alone for a minute without you guys trying to get into some kind of trouble."

Dick then joined him and said, "It is a good thing that Gary was keeping an eye on you two. Otherwise you would have been victims of your first mugging. "

Then Bobby said, "It's time for us to go meet Eddie let's head back to the hotel."

On the way back to the hotel Danny spotted a New York City policeman. He decided he would tell him the story of what had just happened in hopes of preventing it in the future. When he got through relating the story the policeman just looked at us and said,

" Let me get this straight. You two under aged individuals were hanging around the nude bars trying to get in and some guy tried to mug you. Is that what you are trying to tell me?" Both Danny and I nodded in agreement.

The policeman just looked at both of us and said:" If I had a nickel for every underage teenager who has tried to get into those clubs I would be rich. Now get out of my sight."

Needless to say we were surprised by his response. We had expected to say that he would look into it at least. We were disappointed. Instead all he did was pick on us for trying to get into those clubs. There was nothing else we could do. We figured the best thing to do now was to go the hotel with others.

When we got back to the hotel Eddie started in on us. All Danny could say was, "Two country boys in the big city."

It was meant to be a joke. Eddie did not find it funny. He just said, "It is time to get some sleep. Go to your rooms. We will be leaving early in the morning."

When we left the next morning the ride was pretty quiet. All Gary could talk about was the meal they had spent eight dollars on and Danny and myself weren't saying a word. We just looked at each other and smiled. For we had just had an adventure in the big city, and what was even better was that the others were there to protect us. We finally felt like one large family. We knew that the color guard was close now. We knew that everyone of us would protect the others as much as we could. It felt like a very close-knit family. And we liked it.

About a month later I was visiting a friend in a nearby city. There was a parade taking place there that day. I decided to go a watch it. I joined the crowd. It felt funny to me to be a spectator. As I was watching a drum corps approach I heard someone say, "Isn't that color guard the best?"

I turned and asked, "Are you speaking to me?"

The man next to me said, "Yes, I am. Isn't that the best color guard you ever saw?"

I just looked at the man. He had on a jacket from the drum corps that was marching in front of us. Under his name on the jacket was the title of color guard instructor. I just looked at the color guard. I quickly saw four or five things wrong with what they were doing. I saw someone out of step, rifle angles wrong, flag angles wrong, someone looking around, hands not placed properly on the equipment, and someone was out of alignment. I didn't say a word.

The man next to me then said, "Obviously, you don't know anything about drum corps color guards if you don't agree with me that they are the best."

I just turned and walked away. As I was walking away I heard someone ask the man, "Do you know who that was that you were talking to?"

I was to involved in my thoughts to pay any attention. All I could think was that Eddie would have had a field day with that color guard. As I walked I said to myself, "No, sir. I have marched with the best. And that color guard is not it."

About a month later that same man showed up at our practice. He had come to see Eddie to ask him how he could improve his color guard. I just stood there listening while he talked to Eddie. I was glad that he didn't recognize me. I did remember him and I was extremely pleased to see him seeking advice on improving his organization.

When I got home that night I just had to relate that story to Doug. He was amazed. He just looked at me and said: " I guess it true, in the world of the blind the one eyed man is still king,"

And we both just laughed about the whole thing. Again it was our little game. But his response told me that we had definitely astonished him this time.

PART FOUR

Ongoing

The next year once again brought changes for our little color guard. Dick decided that he wanted to leave the drum corps to pursue sports. During the past year he and Bobby had been named to the all-State football team. That fact had stirred an interest him to pursue this endeavor. We did not blame him at all. In fact we were impressed that he felt that passionately about playing football. We could all understand why he did it. And again our line was adjusted. This time Danny was added as a rifleman. Every year someone left and someone else joined our little group. To me it was feeling like a natural thing. I had become closer to these guys than I was to my own brothers. We understood each other and respected each other. We were the only people who truly understood each other. And that fact was important to us all.

The competition season went well for us that year until we got to the Connecticut State championship competition. We had not lost a single competition to that point and Eddie was once again getting nervous over that. The color guard on the other hand just looked at it as just another competition for us to win.

139

When the day came everything was fairly normal for us. We got our equipment ready, got dressed, and went and did our thing on the competition field. After we were coming off the stand Eddie surprised us all. He walked up to Danny and said: " Take your rifle over to individual rifle stand. You are competing there today."

Danny just looked at him and said:" Are you kidding me?"

Eddie just looked at him and said:" No, I am not. Now get over there and get ready to compete."

I walked with Danny to the individual rifle stand. He was nervous, and it was very obvious. All he could say was, " Mike I wish it was you doing this today instead of me."

I looked at him and said," As far as I am concerned the best person is competing today."

His only response was," Thanks a lot friend."

You have to realize that all during the winter practice season Bobby had been working with Danny and I to improve our rifle manual. We had been working hard to get better at it. Bobby kept telling me to take a rifle home with me so I could practice in front of a full-length mirror in order to improve my finger placements. I was still having problems with that. So I had taken his advice and practiced in front of a full-length mirror for an hour everyday. And I was starting to improve. Danny on the other hand had Bobby at home with him constantly going over his rifle manual with him.

We were getting to the Individual rifle stand now. There was a competitor being judged as we got there. This gave Danny a few minutes to gather himself. As he was doing so I checked out his uniform to make sure it was ready.

The judge called his name. I looked him straight in the eyes and asked," Are you ready for this?"

He just looked at me with a very stern look and said:" Let's walk."

I smiled at him and nodded to him just before I stepped aside so he could go on stand to compete. His back was turned to me while he was competing.

I could tell by what I saw that his movements were very clean and crisp. Just before he finished the other members of the color guard showed up. And when Danny was done and walking towards us they all starting applauding and cheering for him. He broke out in a sheepish grin and turned bright red from embarrassment, and said," Let's get out of here so I can get out of this uniform."

We all laughed and accompanied him back to the cars so we could get changed into our street clothes.

When the awards were announced that day we were pleasantly surprised. The drum corps had once again won. Which didn't surprise us at all. We, the color guard had also won. And to top it all off Danny had also won. We were all around him after the announcement congratulating him. I just leaned over to him and said, " See I told you the right person was competing today."

He just smiled and said, " That will be enough out of you. Your day is coming."

And we both smiled.

Our Massachusetts state competition, that year, was at Mountain Park in Holyoke Massachusetts. And once again we prepared for it the way we normally did. Everything was going well that day for us. We felt good about how we had done on the competition field. And as we were walking off the field when Eddie called me over to him. When I got there he said, " Mike take your rifle over to the Individual rifle stand your competing there today."

I just stood there in shock and said," Okay, just don't tell Danny about it okay?"

Then I heard a voice behind be say," To late. Now get your rifle and lets get you to that competition stand." It was Danny.

On the way there I couldn't help myself I just had to say, " I wish it were you doing this today instead of me."

He just looked at me and said," Its your turn in the barrel my friend."

When we got there I was extremely nervous. He spent a lot time trying to calm me down. And when the judge called my name Danny just asked," Are you ready?"

And my response was, "Let's walk."

He stepped aside and let me go the judge to start my entrance into the competition.

I was very nervous at first. I could feel my arms shaking on the first couple of moves. After that they seemed to calm down. And eventually I just did the moves as the judge called them. When it was over the judge saluted me to conclude the competition.

When I turned around the whole color guard was there applauding. And like Danny previously I was embarrassed and could only say, " Let's go get out of these uniforms."

And Danny responded with," See, See how it feels?"

I was feeling pretty proud of the fact that the others had applauded me for my performance. Like Danny, I was embarrassed to have the best I ever new applauding a performance I had done.

And my response was automatic," Thanks a lot, friend."

And we both smiled again.

As it turns out my brother, John was also competing in the individual trumpet at that competition. It was going to be his last year in drum corps. He had been accepted at the University of Notre Dame for the following year. Competing for the individual trumpet was important to him. Unfortunately, he was competing on his competition stand while I was at the individual rifle stand so I didn't get to hear his performance.

The other member of the drum corps told me that he had done a great job and that was all I could rely on.

When the awards were finally announced we were all filled with anticipation. And would you believe it, the drum corps had won again. What is even better our color guard had also won. And then they announced the results of the Individual Rifle. I held my breath. It seemed like it took forever for them to announce the winner. And when then they did. I had won.

The color guard was jumping all over the place. Rushing over to congratulate me. The first one there was Danny all he could say was, " You and me competing against each other in the Northeastern State Championship together. *Yeah.*"

I was ecstatic. I couldn't believe it. Then they announced the Individual trumpet winner. I asked every one to calm down so I could here the announcement. My brother won. I went running to him and when I found him I hugged him and said:" I am proud of you big brother."

He just gave me a big beaming smile and said," I am proud of you to little brother"

And in that moment I understood something. I no longer felt like I had to compete with him. There was no need in it. All I had to do was find my own way. And I had finally found it. There was nothing but mutual respect between us now. He had gone his way and I had finally found mine. It felt good. We both finally understood each other. Both my brother and I couldn't wait to get home to tell our parents how things had worked out. Our mother was completely overjoyed about both of us winning. She just kept telling us how proud she was of the job we had done. From that point on John and I both started working towards competing at the Northeastern State competition.

John had also come with a plan for something that had surprised me. You see it was our parents twenty-fifth wedding anniversary that year. And John thought it would be nice to throw them a surprise anniversary party. Unfortunately John wasn't going to be able to be around for the actual anniversary date. He was scheduled for a school activity for that day. So we had to come up with another way to have the surprise party for them. I told him that I liked that idea and would help him getting it arranged.

The only thing we could think of was to have their friends and relatives come over the house and surprise them. So we started making phone calls to setup the date of our little plan. One disturbing fact kept coming up. The only day the party could take place happened to be the same day as the Northeastern States Competition. When we finally understood that I could only say to him, " It's their anniversary. We don't have to be here for it. We can just go and compete. I am sure they will have a good time without us."

John just looked at me and said, " You know what your right."

And with that we continued planning the party knowing that we were going to be gone that day. At least we wouldn't have to do the dishes that day. Our younger brothers would be stuck with that job instead. And to me that was a good thing.

We left early the day of the competition. It was taking place in Rutland Massachusetts that year. It was a typical Northeastern State Competition with all of the big name drum corps being there. After escorting the drum corps on the musical stand the color guard went off to their competition stand as usual. This process always made me nervous. I still couldn't get over the number of commands we were about to endure to compete.

After we got through Danny and I went looking for the Individual Rifle stand. When we got there I found out that I was to go on first. Danny just looked at me, prior to going on, and asked, " Are you ready?"

My answer was the standard," let's walk."

I was nervous and he knew it. After all this was the Northeastern States Championships we were competing in. And to be identified as the best individual rifleman in the Northeast was quite an honor.

He then stepped aside and I went on to compete.

When it was over for me I went over to him. I looked him straight in the eye and asked," Are you ready for this?"

He just smiled and said," let's walk."

And I stepped aside as he went onto the competition stand. Afterwards we didn't care what happened. We were just glad that it was over. That was one less thing that we had to worry about.

When the awards were announced we found out that the drum corps had once again won. That was really no surprise. They usually did. And we as a color guard had also won. And when the Individual Rifle award was announced Danny and I were standing next to each other. And then they said it. I had won. And he had come in second Danny jumped right into my arms yelling and screaming for me. It felt good. To have one of your closes friends feel that good about what you had done was an amazing feeling.

Then they announce the Individual trumpet winners. And would you believe it, John had won. I ran over to him and give him a hug and said," I guess all those years of playing the scale finally paid off."

He could only smile and say, " I guess you are right."

He was happy. And his smile showed it. He was showing his emotions and I could feel it.

Soon afterwards Eddie came over with the Individual Rifle sheets in his hands. He gave me mine and gave Danny his. As it turned out I had beaten him by only one point. Those marks made me feel much better about it. It was a close competition. And that was all we wanted. Danny and I both hugged each after seeing these marks. We had both done well that day and we knew it.

John and I were both excited to get home and tell our parents that they had two reigning Northeastern Champions in the house. We had completely forgotten about the anniversary party by the time we got home.

When we got into house I couldn't control myself I walked in announcing:" This is now the residence of the Northeastern State Individual trumpet and Individual rifle champions. "

Our mother just looked at us and said: " I am very proud of you two for that. But I am even prouder of what you did for us today. Your Aunts all told us what you two did for that anniversary party."

I just looked at her, pointed at John, and said:" It was all his doing."

She just smiled and walked over and gave us both a hug. Our father just smiled beaming with pride. And to me it felt great. They appreciated what we had done. And to them the most important part was that we had done it together.

The Test

School was changing for me that year. One of our parish priests had become our religion teacher and guidance counselor. His name was Father O'Neal. He was about my height and weight. He had an easygoing demeanor about him. He had dark brown hair and eyes that just lit up when he talked to you. He was a well- respected priest in our parish. Whenever he spoke everyone listened. And yet he was a man of a few words. The thing that impressed me the most about him was that he treated us, the students of the high school, as his equal. This had a major impact on me learning religion. He was willing to discuss it. This was a concept that the nuns would never accept. He was also willing to explain areas that the nuns would never attempt. I was learning that subject for the first time and enjoying it. He was also a smoker. This was good for me. He knew that I smoked and he would often get me out of classes to have a discussion with me as my guidance counselor. Which in our code meant, "let's go have a cigarette."

I never complained about this. My only question to him was, " Can you make our next session during biology. That is one really boring class."

He just looked at me, smiled and said, " I'll see what I can do."

We had become friends. We would often have very candid conversations while we were in the back of the school. He often used me as a frustration dump for some of the other students he was dealing with. He never mentioned any names but to me he didn't have to. He would mention his frustration and I would give him my perspective on the situation. They were very educational conversations for me. I was learning a lot from this man.

During one of these meetings he brought up one of his frustrations that had been bothering him for a while by saying, "You know as a guidance counselor I am learning a lot about your classmates. All the majority of them want to do is become rich and famous some day. And I find that very frustrating."

I just looked at him and smiled. He just looked at me quizzically and said, " Why are you smiling?"

I responded be saying, " Being rich and famous is a double edged sword. Along with fame comes a brand of responsibility that I am almost certain that they don't understand."

He just stood there and looked at me for a few seconds and then said, " You know, Mike when the day comes that you decide to let everyone know what you are capable of I want to be around to see it."

I just looked at him and said, " You will be, and I promise you that." And we went inside so I could complete my biology class.

About a month later the PSAT's (Practice scholastic aptitude test) were scheduled to take place. This test was intended to give the individuals who were planning to attend college and opportunity to practice their skills before taking the actual tests that could be used for college entrance. The nun's were very busy getting people ready for them. When I told them that I wanted to take part in the test they just told me that it would be a waste of my time. Still I told them I definitely wanted to take part in it. At first they continued to tell me that the exercise would be a waste of time for me. I persisted. They talked about it, and they decided let me take the test. They told me that it might do me some good to see just how far behind I was.

This comment didn't bother me. I had decided that it was time for me to show them what I was capable of and I didn't care what they thought.

The test was given in at our local Junior High School. The proctors of the exams explained that each test was unique. No two tests were the same. While I was there I had the opportunity to sign up for additional electives on the test. Each person was given a sheet of paper with elective choices on it. These additional selections would be given in a test format at the conclusion of the general test. So I decided to take the Modern Math II, Physics, and Chemistry electives. These were all classes that I had no exposure to in high school.

I was surprised; the people leading the test let me take the electives I had chosen. I took the tests. I felt good about what I had done. It was an unusual experience for me. Feeling good about anything to do with school was definitely strange for me. I didn't think about it too much after that. Then about a month later I was called down to the principal's office. I had spent a lot of time in the principal's office in the past. For one reason or another. Because of that it didn't bother me to be called down there. I just couldn't figure out what I had done this time.

When I got to her office she told me to sit down in a chair across from her desk. She wore very thick wire rimmed glasses and through them she would lean close to you to speak. I use to think she was trying to intimidate people with this move. But this time it didn't matter. I couldn't think of a thing that I had done, recently, that would warrant this visit. Then she spoke in a very crisp tone, " You are going to sit here until your guidance counselor gets her so we can all discuss something."

I just said to myself, " Okay, at least this way I get out of Biology class again."

We both just sat there staring at each other. I thought she was trying to bore a hole through my mind so she could figure out what I was thinking. I was just being arrogant and sat there, in that hard backed uncomfortable chair, and starred right back at her.

Then my friend the priest came into the office. He just looked at me and said, "Hi Mike."

I responded with, " Hello Father."

Then the principal spoke, " Now that we are through with the greetings I want to discuss why we are all here. Michael, (she always called me that. And I hated it) we got your test scores back for the PSAT test today and we firmly believe that you cheated during the test."

I just sat there and said in amazement," you think I did what?"

I was angry. If nothing else I had always been honest. And there is no way I was going to try to cheat on that test. I didn't have to.

Before anyone could speak she continued, "There is no other way you could have scored near the top of your class without cheating. And there is no way you could have scored as high as you did in your electives without doing something wrong."

My friend the priest was surprised, at first he just sat there absorbing everything she was saying. Then he turned to me, shaking his head and said," Now, you choose now."

I just smiled and said," I sure did."

He then told me to go back to my Biology class and he would come and get me soon. I wasn't about to argue with him. I was getting out of that situation. It was pretty uncomfortable in that room. And I new I didn't cheat on those tests. So I went back to class.

About twenty minutes later he came and got me. We both walked to our usual meeting place. He then spoke to me, " You know that you have just thrown all of those nun's for a complete loop. They thought they had you all figured out. You have been playing with them for years and now they know it. I want to warn you my friend they are going to give you a hard time from here on in. You have finally shown them what you are capable of and now they are going to expect it from you from now on. And by the way there is no way of cheating on that test you took and they know it. They just didn't know how to respond to your scores. I still don't believe that you chose now, but I am glad that you finally decided to show yourself. The only thing is, to me, you did it the hard way."

I just looked at him, smiled and said: " That is the only way I know."

He just smiled and shook his head in response.

Then we both went back into the school so I could once again complete my biology class. I was still angry when I got home from school that day. When I told my mother about the incident she grabbed her coat and said, " That's it. I am going to have chat with that nun about accusing you of cheating. And for once she will not have the upper hand."

It took me twenty minutes to calm her down. She finally understood that Father O'Neal and I had already worked the situation and he had warned me that I was going to have to work harder from now on.

He was right. Things did get tougher with the nuns from that point on. Fortunately, I was prepared. I even did homework and took part in classes from that point on. The time for me to show what I could do was at hand and I was prepared. In fact my grades even showed it.

When the report cards came out I was anxious to bring it home for the first time. My mother just looked at it and smiled. And would you know those familiar words came out of her mouth: " I told you that you could accomplish whatever you decided to do. It is about time."

I just smiled and walked to my room. Regardless of what happened from this point on I had proven her little saying to be true. Of course I would never admit it to her. In fact those words would become my mantra for the rest of my life.

Winter Color Guard

It was during this time that a junior color guard was formed up for the Drum corps.

It was made up of younger boys that could one day become part of the competing color guard. My younger brother Rick was designated as the sergeant of the junior color guard. I was proud of the fact that my brother wanted to take part. Evan though he was still pretty defiant towards me. I figured that if I left him alone he might just do okay at this. Bobby was the one designated as the instructor for the junior color guard and they were good. Of course I was never going to admit this to my younger brother. In our family you only got comments when you did something wrong. The expectations were that you would always do a good job. And therefore it was the family norm. It was something that our mother had engrained into us. And we had all responded in our own ways. Except when it came to games. Then it was all out competition. For us that was fun. Whenever I visited other families I had noticed that there norms on this subject were different. That didn't bother me. After all I came from a family of four boys and my mother had to come up with some way dealing with all of us. And that was her way of coping with it.

During one Thursday practice Eddie called everyone together. He wanted to inform everyone that he had just received a notice about a new type of competition starting up for the winter. It was called Winter Color Guard. The purpose was to give people competition experience before the upcoming summer competition season. Eddie wanted to know if the color guard wanted to compete in this new activity.

Bobby was the first one with a question, "Does it include the drum corps?"

Eddie told them, "No, these competitions were setup strictly for the color guards only. You compete in individual saber, individual rifle, and individual flag manual."

It took Bobby about three seconds to formulate a response. "That might be a good place for the junior color guard to get some experience."

Eddie just smiled and said, "I agree, some of us will go to see what these competitions are all about. And our junior color guard will compete."

So it was decided. My brother Rick was going to compete in the individual saber, and individual rifle, while other members of the junior color guard were going to compete in individual flag manual. Needless, to say my younger brother, Rick, was surprised. Bobby just told him not to worry; he would work with him to get ready.

On the day of the competition Rick and I both rode with Eddie. This gave me a chance to speak to my younger brother. I said the following to him, " Rick, remember you are going to compete against seasoned veterans today. So I would not expect a whole lot if I were you."

Rick's response really didn't surprise me. He just looked at me and said, "I am a member of the Whip City color guard. And there is only one way for me to go. And that is to win."

I just looked at him and thought to himself, "My god, he has already accepted the philosophy. And I sure hope that you can backup that defiance little brother."

When we got there the experienced members of the competing color guard were not impressed with the setup. We definitely preferred the summer competition activities. My brother went on stand for individual saber first.

After that he went straight to the individual rifle stand. During this time the others went to the individual flag stand. It took about three hours for the competition to be over and another hour for them to total up all of the scores.

When they finally did make the announcements I was surprised. Rick had taken first place in individual saber and individual rifle. And the others had come in first and second in the individual flag manual. They all received medals. Rick and the other members of the junior color guard were excited. They couldn't control their emotions. They just jumped up and down yelling with excitement. It took a few minutes of celebrating before they were once again in control of their emotions. When I went over to congratulate my brother he only had one thing to say, "Do you want to talk about those seasoned veterans now?"

I just smiled and said, "No, I don't think we need to discuss them at all, do you?"

I had gained a new respect for him that day. He was defiant, I will give him that, but he had a right to be that way. He had just beaten some of the best competitors in the Northeast. He deserved it. We both just smiled at each other. I was extremely proud of him that day. I didn't have to tell him. He knew by the look that I gave him.

That day belonged to the junior color guard. They finally knew what it felt like to compete and win. This was their day. Eddie and the others didn't say a word except to congratulate them.

On the way home the junior color guard members all wanted to ride together. Once this was arranged that left the experienced member of the color guard riding in Eddie's car. They talked about the winter guard competitions.

Bobby put it best when he said, "Well, that definitely tells you something when our junior color guard members, who had never competed before, can beat seasoned veterans in individual competition. This type of competing doesn't seem like anything I would want to take part in."

The rest of us all agreed. Except Eddie did add that the junior color guard did well that day and he was proud of them.

A Change

We were now in fall season or what we called the practice season. The time when everyone in the color guard was working on perfecting their skills for the upcoming competition season. It was also the time for the members to relax a little bit and enjoy each other's company outside of marching.

It was normal for them to congregate at our house a couple of times a month. We were all close now and we treated each other that way. We would spend hours together on our front porch just talking about whatever came into our minds. After all, the things we had been through together the past couple years, had brought us all real close. We were only comfortable saying whatever we wanted with each other. We understood each other. And that is something our other friends couldn't say. Even Doug got involved with everyone, and he enjoyed it. He was having fun along with the rest of us.

Eddie was there with us. He was becoming more than an instructor to us. He was becoming a confident and mentor to all of us.

We would often spend the whole afternoon playing pool in our basement. Your see our Dad had bought us a small pool table and we were getting proficient with it. Billy was the pool shark we had to worry about. Gary believed that he could beat him. He never did. And as a doubles team Danny and I could not be beaten. We had a lot of fun together during that time. If we weren't playing pool we were all sitting on the front porch just talking about whatever came into our minds. It was always interesting, and fun. We constantly picked on each other about our girl friends. Bobby was very close to someone he had met recently and he was excited that their relationship was going real well. Needless to say we all picked on him for that.

You see in our little group no one was safe from getting picked on. We believed that if we knew about it we could pick on you for it. It was always meant in fun and we all knew it.

Then one Sunday evening I got a call from Eddie. The only thing that Eddie could say was: "Bobby is dead. He and his girl friend were parking in Springfield and they were both murdered."

I was in shock. I could barely speak. I forced words out my mouth: "What? Are you kidding me?"

Eddie responded by saying that he was not kidding it was all over the news.

I thanked Eddie for calling and fell into a deep state of shock in front of the television as the news media spoke of the incident over and over again. Doug and Billy were right there with me. We just couldn't believe it. Bobby. It didn't make any sense to us at all.

It took a couple of days for everyone to get over the shock of what happened. Billy was over our house every day waiting for any word on what was going to happen next. We were all completely shattered emotionally. All I could think of was,"

Why? Why Bobby?" It just didn't make any sense to me. My parents were constantly trying to console us. But like in the past, when the two six-month olds died in front of me, it wasn't working. Instead I was once again trying to bury my emotions deep inside me. It was harder this time. Those emotions kept coming back. No matter what I did I couldn't control them. And yet, I new that I was going to have to control these emotions one way or another. It hurt. It felt like someone had torn part of life away from me. And yet I knew that his brothers needed our help. I knew how much they had to be hurting because of this.

As it turned out the color guard were the pallbearers for Bobby's funeral, and people came from all over New England to show their respect. All of the Drum Corps leaders throughout New England were there out of respect for Bobby. This outpouring from other drum corps people just made us all feel good. We knew how they all felt about him. Carrying that casket was one of the most difficult things I had ever done in my life. I just couldn't believe that Bobby was in that casket. And then I would look at Billy and Gary

and the pain and sorrow in their eyes was heartbreaking. All of us ended up in tears while we were carrying that casket. And I don't think anyone cared.

My brother John once again played for the funeral. During the playing of taps none of the color guard could hold back crying. A friend, a brother, and our leader was gone.

After the funeral we were all invited back to the Grover's house. For the whole family new how much Bobby meant to us. It was here that something different happened. Gary, Billy, Danny, Dick, and I were all standing outside not saying a word. When Billy spoke and said, "I pity the color guards we compete against for the next couple of years. I am dedicating the next couple of seasons to Bobby's memory."

They all just looked at each other and one by one nodded in agreement.

About two weeks later Eddie came to practice with a trophy that stood about four feet tall. He then called the corps together and said, "I want to explain something to you. This trophy, and he pointed to the one on the floor next to him, is the Robert Grover Memorial trophy in memory of Bobby. From this point on it will be given to the color guard with the highest marks at the Massachusetts State competition. This includes both junior and senior color guards."

Then I said, "Your not making it easy for us are you?"

Before Eddie could answer, Billy said, "That is our way isn't it?"

And the whole color guard smiled and nodded. As the next year came along there was only one thing on our minds. That was to win the Robert Grover memorial trophy. After all he was one of us. And it meant everything to us.

When the Massachusetts State Championship came along that year winning that trophy was our only thought. And when the awards where given out we had done it. We won the trophy and our name would be the first one to be placed on the placard on the side of it. And that meant everything to us. That is all we wanted to do that day. And we had succeeded.

When the Northeastern championships came around that year we were ready for it. The competition took place in New York again that year. So once again we had to leave early to get there on time.

Once we got there we were all business. We just dove straight into preparing for the competition. We inspected and cleaned all of our equipment with a renewed drive to get it all absolutely perfect.

The judge for the color guard competition that year was from the New York Association. He was well known for being very tough and fair. That was our kind of judge.

When we got to the stand we got a good look at him. He was a stocky man dressed in a VFW (Veterans of foreign wars) uniform with a garrison cap on. He stood about five feet ten inches and had a very intimidating stare when he was judging someone. He did demonstrate that he was knowledgeable and that made us feel good.

We liked being judged by someone who knows what he is doing. We just knew that we would be judged fairly that day. And that was all that we asked.

Just before we stepped off to compete Gary came around to each one of us and asked"

Are you ready for this?"

And our answer to his question was consistently," For Bobby."

Once he had checked out each one of us he stepped out in front where he could see all of us, with a very strong look on his face, and said, " For Bobby."

He did a quick about face and marched us to the competition stand. The judge was taking forever that day. It seemed like he was using a magnifying glass for each movement. Every movement seemed like it took longer than I had remembered from the earlier Northeastern competitions I had been in. And then it was over.

After the judge gave his final salute he turned to walk away. He suddenly stopped, turned around towards Gary and said," That was absolutely beautiful." And walked away.

Gary just nodded to him in response and marched us off to the cars to get changed.

As it turned out Danny had won the Massachusetts Individual Rifle Championship title that year and was competing for the Northeastern title that day. I accompanied him to the stand and watched as he competed. Since I had won last year Eddie felt that it was Danny's turn to try to get a Northeastern title. And I was happy to see him compete instead of me. I still remembered going through that experience the year prior with extreme nervousness. When he got off I could only say to him," I am glad I am not competing with you this year. That was amazing to watch."

He just looked at me and said," That was for Bobby."

He didn't have to say anymore. I completely understood and he new it.

We were pretty quiet while we were waiting for the awards that day. We had put all of our emotions on the competition stand. There was nothing left. And sure enough we won. What is even better Danny won Individual rifle. We didn't celebrate much, all we did was look at each other and say, " For Bobby." That was all we needed to say.

From that point on it became important for us to continue winning the Robert Grover Memorial trophy. After all Bobby was one of the people who had inspired us for the drive to perfection.

The next year Danny left the color guard to join the Military. He had graduated from High school and joined the Marine Corps within a month afterwards. This was a real blow for me. One of my closes friends was not going to be marching with me anymore. I was going to miss him marching in the line with us. But I had gotten accustomed to friends moving on with their lives and it had become part of the yearly color guard activity. That was the only way for us to grow by bringing in new members and I knew it. Even though I knew it, his leaving did hurt.

But the quest for the Robert Grover Memorial trophy went on. And during that year we won it again. Then winning that trophy became an obsession to us. It became more important to the color guard than the Northeastern States Championship.

During the following year we learned that Danny had died while serving in Viet Nam.

This information was devastating to me. I didn't know how to deal with it. I had lost another part of me with that information. It was another close part, a part I had treasured.

To loose a friend when you could say goodbye was one thing. But to loose a close friend that you would never have a chance to say goodbye to that was something else. I was having a hard time with Danny's death.

And the only thing that seemed to help was competing. It was the only way I could think of to express myself that would honor his memory. My emotions were being driven deep inside me again and I knew it.

Another dedication was made in Danny's memory for the upcoming season and the

Robert Grover Memorial trophy. And we continued to win everything that year including the trophy. And the drive to continue that trend motivated every member of the color guard. We all remembered Danny. And his loss meant a lot to all of us. We no longer competed just for ourselves. Now it was in the memory of Bobby and Danny. And that fact was important to all of us. This was the way we chose to honor their memory. By doing what they did so well, in their memory, meant a lot to all of us that year.

I was attending a technical school in New Britain Connecticut during the next two years. The proximity of school allowed me to continue competing. As school came to a close for me I enlisted in the Army with a departure date right after graduation.

This departure date of mine landed right in the middle of the competition season that year. So Eddie and I both decided that it would be best if I didn't compete and helped him instructing instead. That was a strange feeling for me. Not being able to compete that year was a hard pill to swallow. I was still learning for Eddie that year. We all were. After all he was the best color guard instructor in the Northeast and we all new it. And to have the opportunity to instruct with him was a great lesson. I had to leave for basic training before the competition season started that year. Before leaving I did address the color guard to remind them of what Bobby and Danny had meant to me. Along with that I told them what I expected them to do during the competition season that year. And then I left the practice with tears in my eyes.

The Legacy

It turned out that the Whip City Drum Corps color guard won the Robert Grover Memorial trophy for a total of fifteen consecutive years. To them this meant a lot. True their color guard's name was put on the side of that trophy for fifteen years. But that didn't mean as much to them as the actual winning of the trophy dedicated to one of their fellow members did.

Every year someone left the color guard for one reason or other, some to go to school, others to take part in school athletics, and others to join the military. Every year there were new members and yet every year the color guard continued to win because of the memory of they're past leaders.

People come and go in the color guard. Those that left usually did well. After all we had all learned about teamwork, continuous improvement, and pride long before the American business community had any concept of these items. I was also very proud of the fact that my two younger brothers Rick and Joe had also joined the color guard and continued to carry on the inspirations provided by the four Grover brothers.

Whenever you win a championship for one year everyone says that you had a great year. When you win that same championship two years in a row they start talking about you being a champion. When you win the same title five years in a row you a considered on the verge of becoming a legend. When you win the same championship ten years in a row you are designated a legend. And when you win the Northeastern States Championship seventeen consecutive years like this color guard did you are considered an icon.

I had spent seven years competing with the color guard. And after three years in the military, I instructed the color guard for another six years. And I was proud of every moment that I had spent with that organization. When the time came for me to leave it was difficult. Even today the reasons for my leaving still haunt me. But the knowledge that I was part of something great has always stayed with me. Besides that I have definitely learned that doing things the hard way is not always the wrong way for me.

We all learn in different ways. For me it turned out that I could only learn by doing things the hard way. And the knowledge of this fact is still with me today.

PART FIVE

Reflections

It was now eight years after I had gone into the military. Doug and I were standing at the starting point of another Memorial Day parade in Westfield. The reason we were together was that Doug's wife, who happened to be my cousin Denise, had talked to my mother and found out that I was going to be there with the drum corps that day. This was the first time we had seen each other in five years.

Doug asked, "So how are you doing now?"

I didn't know what he was referring to at first. Then it came to me. Doug knew that I was going through something emotional, and he was trying to help. It turns out that both Doug and I had spent time in the Army during the Viet Nam conflict. When I left the Army I no longer wore my emotions on my sleeve. Instead I was once again holding them inside me. Deep inside me. These were emotions that I never wanted to have come out.

There are a lot of things for an individual to learn in the military. One of the main ones is how to deal with fear. It is something you often get to deal with a lot in the Army. And the military method of dealing with it is to teach you to react and not think of it. That concept works for that moment only. It really doesn't hit you until afterwards. And Doug knew, by looking at me, that this was my afterwards.

The time when all of my emotions were coming at me was at hand. And he could tell. I was struggling to deal with them and he knew it. He had seen it before and totally understood the meaning.

After getting out of the Army I had moved back to Westfield and got a job with a local computer company. After all I did have some pretty in depth electronics training from the Technical school had attended. And it was time to put that education to work.

Things had worked out well for me in that job. I was introducing new products for this company. This activity left me on the road most of the time. It was time for me to be alone with my emotions. A time that I could try to control them by shoving them deep inside of me. No matter what I did, or how did it, they still came up. All of the fear and insecurity of being in a potential hazardous situation just kept coming up more and more. I had to deal with it and I knew it. I just wasn't sure how. And while I was alone I started to understand. I remembered the trance, which was really a form of meditation, which we used to enter into while marching. And I found myself using it to heal some of my wounds.

The people that I worked for had even allowed me to hire and train my own team. I was able to find one strong person in each discipline that would be required to introduce the product we were working on. And they were a great team.

When I got home from the military I had some surprises waiting for me. My younger brother Rick was now in the competition color guard. And I was proud of him for that.

What was even more surprising was that Rick now stood over six feet tall and referred to me as *his* "little brother." This bothered me at first. My only response was to repeat what John had always said to me," I am your older brother and *not you're little brother*." Saying this would always remind me of John used to say it to me. And it felt good to hear myself say them.

After my brother John had graduated from Notre Dame he had gone into the Navy.

As it turned out he had graduated number three in his class as an Electrical Engineer. To me that was impressive. To him it just wasn't quite good enough. He would have been a lot happier if he had graduate number one in his class. I just looked at that as John being John. He was stationed in Washington, D.C. He had a great job. He was on the personal staff of an Admiral. His responsibilities in this job were classified. Which meant that he could tell no one about what he was working on. Not even us, the members of his family. He was also going for his master degrees in Electrical Engineering, Physics, and nuclear Engineering at Georgetown University. Entering three masters degree programs at once was something that only he would attempt. I just couldn't believe anyone could have that kind of ambition to attempt that. Unfortunately, John's habit of not letting out his emotions had finally caught up to him. He had a psychotic breakdown. He was in a Veteran's Hospital in Boston for recovery. When I went to see him he was half of the man I remembered. He had a hard time communicating with me. He struggled for words to express himself.

Don't get me wrong he was happy to see me. And I was happy to see him. But to see a man with so much potential be reduced to what he was broke my heart. What was even worse he had just been told that the Navy had just retired him. And the thing that really disturbed him was that he would never return to the person he once was. I knew that I loved him and now I was willing to say it. And when I did it felt good.

I just kept remembering how I used to compete with him when we were growing up. And how he always held everything in. I decided right then and there that it was time that I wore my emotions on my sleeve again. From then on anybody could always tell how I was feeling. And it felt good to start letting them out again. My brother had once again had a major influence on me, and once again it was going to help me. John would never again be the person he once was. That was a given. We all had to learn from this. Even me. And I was learning from his experience. I had always known that John holding his emotions in was not a good thing. And now the results of that were right in front of me and I could not allow it to happen to me.

I was now standing with my younger brothers and they wanted to tell me everything they had been doing for the past couple of years. Rick was excited to tell me about how the color guard had been doing since I had gone into the Army. It turned out that they had continued their winning ways.

In fact Rick and another member, named Dan, had also continued the legacy of winning the Northeastern Individual rifle championships. I just asked one question, " Who has been winning the Robert Grover memorial Trophy?" It still meant a lot to me and Rick knew it.

Rick just looked me in the eye and said, " Why us of course. Who else would win it?"

I just looked at him and said, "Good." To myself I said, " Still a little defiant I see."

Rick then told me that Gary was instructing the guard now and I should come down practice some Thursday and say hello.

I did. I was really pleased to see Gary. It felt real good. We hugged each other when I first got there. I just sat there and watched as the color guard practiced. And remembered just how good it felt to be part of that unit.

I felt nothing but pride watching them practice that day.

After the practice Gary came over to me to tell now good it was to have me there.

He told me that I was welcome to come to their practices anytime. I did visit quite a bit that year. Whenever I needed a little grounding. Watching them practice was very calming to me.

At the end of that competition season that year Gary decided he had to leave instructing the color guard. They had once again won everything and he felt that it was time for him to move on. On one of my visits to their practice the Corp's director came up to me and asked to speak with me after practice.

I said:" Sure,"

After all I still considered him a good friend. And I had nothing but respect for him.

When the practice was over the director approached me with the following question, " Mike, with Gary leaving as the color guard instructor, and your brother

Rick getting ready to go college next year, would you consider taking over as the Color guard instructor?"

I was surprised to say the least. I knew that since Rick was going to college my presence might help with the continued growth of the color guard. I also knew that I would welcome the chance to use all the instructing techniques that I had learned from Eddie. And for the first time I had to admit that I felt that I owed this organization something for what they had taught me. I just wasn't sure if I was the right person to do it. But I was one of the people who contributed to the success of the color guard at one time. And because of that I thought that I might just be able to teach others what I had learned during that experience.

I just looked at the director and said: "Yes."

The next year was a challenging one for me. For when Rick went to college all of the

other members of the color guard also left for one reason or another. They were all the same age and they all felt it was time for them to move on to school or the military. That left me with starting a brand new color guard with no experience. We did have a ten-man color guard, that year, and that part excited me. Something else that excited me was that my youngest brother Joe was in the color guard now. He had been a part of the Drum line for a couple of years and decided that he wanted to be part of the color guard.

I was extremely proud of that.

The new Sergeant was a young man named Mark. Both he and his brother John had joined the color guard together. The new lead rifleman was named Scott. I was impressed with Mark and Scott. I had seen a lot of leadership potential in both of them and I could see them growing as they continued their training. We had to spend a lot of time on basics that year. I constantly found myself parroting Eddie words: " You are going to do this until you can't do it wrong."

At first it felt funny to me to be using Eddie's philosophy. But then I was able to rationalize it by saying to myself: " It is a proven process. And it works."

And besides that I really enjoyed seeing them get better with each practice. It was a learning experience for me and I was enjoying each moment of it.

As we got ready for the season I knew that they weren't quite where they needed to be. We had practiced as often as we could but with a completely new color guard it takes time to get them where they need to be.

I also knew that with experience they would improve. I just had rely on the fact that once the season started they would continue learning.

That competition season was not a good one for the color guard until they got to the

Connecticut State Championship competition. And would you believe it, they won. I was beside myself with pride for the new color guard. That had come together at the right time. The only thing I had to worry about was the ego's getting ahead of them.

The following week they competed in Thomaston Connecticut. The only way I could describe their performance was, dreadful, at the least. And the thing that I was afraid of had happened. Their egos got the best of them. They felt that since they were the Connecticut State Champions that no one could beat them. Boy did they have a hard lesson to learn.

When they came off the stand I was waiting for them. I brought them to where the cars where parked and proceeded to yell at them for forty minutes about how bad they were. All during this tirade I consistently told them that they needed to have some pride in what they were doing. And they did NOT continue the legacy with that performance. I knew I was being hard on them. But at the same time I felt they needed it. Besides that, my emotions were running in high gear and I was having trouble controlling them. I had never seen a performance from the color guard that was that bad. And I wasn't afraid to let them know that. They had violated one of Eddie's rules and I wasn't going to let them forget it. You see I still remember Eddie telling us that there was no room for egos in that organization. That day I had seen the results of that happening. And I wasn't going to allow it to happen again.

From that point on Scott took it on himself to say something before they stepped off for every competition.

His statement was always the same, " Don't forget a meet called Thomaston."

After the Thomaston incident I decided that I had to do something different to prepare them for the upcoming Massachusetts State championship competition. The approach I chose to make was to make their timing reactive. What that meant was that they would no longer spend time thinking about the moves. Instead they would just perform them. The way I chose to do this surprised them. We were having our double practices on Tuesday evenings. I started by changing our practice location to the local trade school. They were surprise with the location change but they had learned to accept my quirks in training.

When we all got there I asked Mark to take the flag line into an adjoining room and to start working on their timing. I then told each rifleman to stand in a different corner of the gymnasium. Once they did this I told them to turn around so they were each looking at different corner. Once they did this I told them close their eyes. About now they were completely confused. But they did it anyways.

I then went into the center of the gymnasium and said the following, " The key to rifle manual is timing. The timing of this group has been very erratic. We are going to work on improving your timing by teaching you to listen. "

This comment definitely through them off balance, and they all turned and looked at me. I told them, " Just turn back around, close your eyes and listen." And then I gave the command for them to go to right shoulder. Once they got there I asked them: " How many rifles did you hear?"

The answers I got back ranged from three to two. The response didn't surprise me. I then told them that we were going to practice this way until we could hear one rifle for each move. After about and hour of this their timing started improving. In fact about half way through it I started getting a pleasant surprise. Every time I would ask how many rifles they heard Scott would tell me the exact person that was late with the movement. And then I new that he was starting to get it. He understood how important it was to listen.

We practiced like this for the first hour of the next couple of weeks. The second hour we spent as a total unit. It was working. Mark had worked wonders with the flag line and Scott was having more and more of an impact with the riflemen. He would have them go off by themselves and just work on the timing with their eyes closed until he could hear only one rifle.

As the competition season continued that year I was pleasantly surprised. They had only won three competitions that year. The Connecticut State Championship, The Massachusetts State Championship, and the Northeastern State's Championships. And they had also retained the Robert Grover Memorial Trophy. Besides that, Scott had won his first Northeastern State's individual rifle championship. I was proud of them all and I told them so.

During the off-season I could see the whole color guard coming together more and more. I couldn't believe how much Mark reminded me of Bobby. His actions where the same, the way he carried himself, his concern for the other members of the guard, his ability to teach, they were all a reminder of Bobby. And he loved life like Bobby did.

The following season was a surprise to us. During the off season every year the individual drum corps associations would have their meetings to discuss potential rule changes for the upcoming competition season. Each drum corps had one representative at each of these meetings. Whenever a new rule change was brought up it would be introduced at one meeting and voted on at the next one.

This year a new rule was proposed for the color guard competitions. They called it the flag ratio system. The way it worked was simple. If your color guard had ten flags in it you would receive a tenth of a point off for every mistake the color guard made. For every additional member of the flag line you would have less and less taken off of your total score. Basically the points taken off, whenever you did something wrong were proportional to the number of flag bearers you had in your color guard over ten. The intention of this rule, to me, was to aid the larger color guards so they could be more competitive. This rule did not help us any. We only carried the American flag and four saluting flags at any one time.

When our representative told me about it I told him that I wanted to attend the next meeting to argue against it. You see I didn't believe that the flag line alone should be the determining factor for the whole color guard. To me it made more sense to utilize this ratio system for the whole color guard not just the flag line. To me it should be considered one complete unit.

When we got to the meeting I was surprised that they opened up the proposal to the floor for discussion. I got up and tried to make my case. Another person got up immediately after me and said, " We all know that when some one joins a color guard they always start in the flag line.

It takes a long time for someone to become good at this. With this ratio system we have an opportunity to retain them as members instead of discouraging them like we do now. This flag ratio system will allow us to maintain members and continue growing our organizations."

I had to think about what he said. I didn't totally agree with him. He did have a valid point. But to me it was up to the instructors to keep their color guard members interested and growing. After all Eddie had ensured that we always knew every part of the color guard and to me that worked.

When the vote came the rule was changed. There was nothing I could do about it then. Before I left the meeting one of the instructors for another color guard came up to me and said," That settles it. You guys don't have a prayer to dominate again this year."

I just looked at him and thought to myself," We'll see."

You have to understand that through the years we had heard that statement a lot. And up until now no one had been able to do it. We had always maintained our winning record regardless of what our opponents had done to impact it. And that meant a lot to us.

When we got to the practice the following week I explained the outcome of the meeting to the color guard. Their response surprised me. Mark and Scott just looked at me and Mark said," I don't see what difference it is going to make for us. We'll just do what we have always done. We'll just have to be better at it."

All I could do was smile in response. He had gotten the philosophy. He understood what it was all about, for this color guard.

Then the competitions season started. And before the color guard stepped off for the first one, Scott had only one thing to say to the other members, "Remember a meet called Thomaston."

When the competition was over that day we had come in second. We had lost by a tenth of a point to a color guard that had ten saluting flags and one rifle. We just chalked that competition up to experience and decided to work even harder for the next one.

When the next competition came along I was surprised again. It turned out that whenever we were getting ready members of some of the other color guards that we were competing against walked around counting how many flags we were going to use that day. This information was then used to determine how many they would use. If you had five flags out like we did. They would make sure that they fielded at least ten flags that day to ensure their success. I didn't think much of this at first. To me it was the performance of the whole color guard that mattered. Not just the flag line.

When the awards came out that day we had taken second place again. And again we were defeated by a tenth of a point.

And then one of the instructors, of one of the other color guards that we competed against, came up to me and said," We warned you that you wouldn't be able to dominate this year. If you want to continue winning you are going to have to conform to our way of doing things. Or we will drive your color guard into oblivion"

I didn't say anything to him. I just thought to myself:" We'll see."

I couldn't get his comments out of my mind. I just kept thinking that there has to be a way for us to get our point across. And then I came up with it.

It had come to me all at once. It was something that no had tried before. At least from what I remembered no one had tried it.

The Connecticut State Championship competition was coming up soon and that was were I intended on putting my plan in place. Prior to practicing, one Thursday night, I pulled Mark and Scott aside and told them my plan. The plan was simple. Instead of trying to compete with the flag ratio system we would demonstrate how important the whole color guard was by fielding only rifles for the upcoming Connecticut State Championship.

Mark was the first to respond by saying, " I love it. You want to take the most difficult aspect of the color guard and demonstrate how it should be done by the whole unit."

I hadn't thought of it that way. But he was right. Scott loved it also. And then we started practicing with nothing but rifle manual to get ready. And we practiced until we couldn't get it wrong. Not a new concept for this group.

When the competition came a pleasant surprise was presented to us.

The judge that day was the leading Individual rifle judge in Connecticut. He was someone who knew as much as we did about rifle manual and that impressed us. We had nothing but respect for him as a judge.

We had to march in a parade for the initial part of that competition. And the stand portion of the activity was to take place immediately following the parade. As we were getting ready I noticed members of our opposing color guards walking around and decided to have some fun with them. I had our color guard put all seven of our flags out as if we were preparing them for the competition.

The results of this action were exactly what I expected. They counted how many flags we had out and went running back to their instructors to inform them of what they thought we were planning to do.

As we got ready for the parade we were all nervous. No one had ever tried what we were about to do. Not even the color guards that I was in had tried this one. Before they stepped off I told them how proud I was of them for trying this. And then I left to watch them as they competed in the parade phase of the competition. I couldn't wait to see what was going to happen.

As the parade got started I went ahead to where the judge was to try to get a feel as to how they were doing when they marched by the judging stand. When the color guard got the judging point the crowd, which was mainly filled with drum corps people, went completely silent. And then I started hearing comments. They were all the same. The other drum corps people kept saying," You have got to be kidding. No one in their right mind would try competing with nothing but rifles. There is no way possible to be competitive that way. Especially with that flag ratio system."

All I could do was smile.

From the parade they went directly to the competition stand. And again when they went on the stand something unusual happened. The crowd was completely quiet. Not a sound was heard. They just stared it amazement. All during the competition I just watched as the color guard performed beautifully. And when the competition was over the crowd went wild with cheers. I couldn't believe how loud they were. I could barely hear myself think with all of the noise.

Then from my left side I heard some one calling my name. It was the judge and he said," Mike I have to tell you something. I have been judging rifle manual for a long time and that performance I just saw was flawless. A complete color guard of rifles, your color guard is the only one who could pull that off. I am telling you right now that if you don't win this competition I will personally lead the effort to remove the flag ratio system for next year. There is no way you should lose this competition."

I just looked at him and said, " Thank you. I am real proud of what the color guard did today." I then walked off to tell them how I felt about their performance.

When the awards came out we had once again come in second. We were once again beaten by a tenth of a point. It turns out that we had one thing marked against us during the parade while the on stand performance was perfect. And guess who came to see me before we left that day.

It was the judge and he said," There is no way you should have lost with that performance today. That flag ratio system **will** be voted out this year."

We were excited. We had taken on the established powers in that association and, in our minds, beaten it. And we did it our way. Namely the hard way.

Myself, my brother Joe and one other member of the color guard were putting the equipment away after a competition one day when a young woman dressed in a color guard uniform came up to me. She just looked at me and asked, " I am here to find out when I can become a member of this color guard. I have been marching for two years now and I want to join you guys."

I just looked at her. I then turned to my brother and said, " Hand me that rifle."

He did and I handed it to the young lady. When she tried to grab it the rifle went right to the ground. And she said, "It's heavy."

I took the rifle from her and said, " I see you have a flag cup on why don't we try one of those."

She looked confidently at me and said," Okay, I can do that."

I then asked my brother to hand me one of our flags. Once he handed it to me I gave it to the young lady. And said:" Bring it up to the Right Shoulder position."

She struggled. She couldn't get the flag up high enough to place it into flag cup. She gave me back the flag and said:" It's too heavy."

I looked at her and said, " These items are the equipment that we use in this color guard.

She just looked at me and said," You will just have to get lighter equipment so I can join. All the other color guards have gotten lighter equipment. Why can't you?"

My response to her was, " If we did that we would no longer be the Whip City color guard."

She just looked at me, jutted out her jaw, stomped her right foot and said, "You're just a male chauvinist pig."

And then she walked away.

I was amazed at her response. My youngest brother walked over to me laughing and said," I had told her that she would not like the answer you would give her to that question."

I just looked at him and said," You mean you new about this and you didn't warn me. Well, at least with her going off and telling everyone that I am a chauvinist there won't be any more of your groupies coming over to join us."

And we both thought it was funny. Unfortunately I was wrong. The next week three other young women came over to me at three different times that day asking the same question. When I handed the first two the flag they also couldn't put the flag into the flag cup. And they both walked a way frustrated. The third one surprised me. She got the flag into the flag holder, and she was holding the flag correctly. Then a gust of wind came up and she almost fell over from the pressure. She didn't say a word. She just took the flag out of the flag holder and handed it to me. And without speaking she just turned and left. After that there were no other requests of that nature.

When we got to the Northeastern States competition that year the people who had won the Connecticut State Championship were in for a surprise. You see this competition did not recognize the flag ration system at all.

That definitely put them at a disadvantage with their ten saluting flags that day. Needless to say we won that day and it felt good. To me it felt like the old color guard was back.

During that season three judges approached me with the same comment. It went something like this, " Mike, I have got to tell you something. I am not impressed with your methods, but no one in drum corps can question your results. That color guard that you are teaching is fantastic."

You see whenever our color guard moved. It moved in marching formation. While the other color guards just walked as a group to the competition stand and milled around until they went on the stand.

What I had our color guard do was march up to the competition stand. And then I had them stand at attention while they were waiting for their turn to compete. To me it helped them focus on the task at hand. To other color guard instructors it was an unnecessary activity that they would never attempt. And yet for us it worked and I was not about to change it because they didn't agree with it.

I would only look at them and say: " Thank you." To myself I would think: " You must have been at Thomaston and overheard me yelling."

It was also during this season that the long time director of the drum corps decided to retire. As it turned out Mark's father, who absolutely loved the drum corps because of how it had helped his sons, decided that he would take over. And he did.

The following year had the same winning results. Of course the flag ratio system was removed and we were back to our winning ways. I firmly believed that we had done it. We had once again become the consummate Whip City color guard.

During a practice in the middle of the summer the Drum Corps director asked to speak to me. He started off by saying:"

Mike, I have come into some proof that one of your color guard members was drinking bear at the last competition."

My response was quick, " What? They all know better. I review all of the rules with them every year. That is one that I go over multiple times. Who was it? I want to know."

He just looked at me and said, " I will give you the name. But first remember it is your color guard. You do what you think is right about it. I know how hard your people have worked to get where they are today. Let me know by the end of practice what you decide to do and I will go along with whatever you decide."

Before leaving he did give me the name of the individual. And he emphasized that he did have proof if I needed it. My response to him was," I don't need the proof. And I will let you know what I decide by the end of tonight's practice."

As I was going back to the practice area for the color guard I was beside myself with anger over this issue. After all the work these guys had done to get to where they are and this individual jeopardizes it. I just couldn't believe that one of these guys would do this to the color guard. By the time I got back to the color guard my decision was done. When I got in the same room with them I asked the individual to speak to me in private.

We both walked outside. I then told him the following," We have proof that last week you were drinking beer at the competition."

He didn't say a word. He just stood there with his mouth wide open. I continued," Now you all know the rules. Because of that rule you can no longer march with this color guard. I suggest you leave now without any embarrassment in front of the rest of the members."

He just bowed his head. Nodded. And turned and left. I then went and talked to the director of the Drum Corps. After I told him what I had done he just looked at me and said," You did the right thing. I would have understood if you wanted to disregard that rule in this case. But instead you did the right thing. "

At the end of practice that week I explained what happened to the rest of the color guard. My closing statement to them was, " Rest assured, winning record or not, if someone breaks one of those rules they will be gone. Now have a good week and I will see you at the next practice."

I really didn't think too much of this incident afterwards. As far as I was concerned it was settled. Then about two days later I heard a knock at my door. When I answered it there was the young man that I had just thrown out of the color guard with his mother.

She was a tall woman with a booming voice. We looked eye to eye with me and she was angry. After I invited them in she started to unleash her tirade on me. She started by saying," How dare you embarrass my son that way? He loves this color guard and you throw him out for something he didn't do?"

All during this I was watching the young man. He was having a hard time. He kept looking down at our floor. He couldn't even look me straight in the eye. It took me a few minutes to calm the mother down. When I finally did she was willing to listen to my suggestions. I told her," I will gladly discuss this whole subject with you after I discuss it with your son. And if you are willing to wait outside so he and I could have a quick conversation with him I will come out and tell you If I need to apologize publicly to your son for the embarrassment I might have caused him. In fact if I am wrong I will reinstate him into the color guard no questions asked."

She just looked at me and said," As long as you do the right thing by him."

And she went outside to sit in her car for few minutes while her son and I talked. After she left I stood there watching the young man. He was still staring at the floor. I then said to him," I meant what I said to your mother. I will reinstate you if I am wrong."

Without raising his head he said," I know. You usually don't say things you don't mean."

I looked at him and said," You know it really doesn't matter what I think. The only thing that really matters is if you have been honest with yourself.

Without being honest with yourself you have nothing to stand on for the future. Have you been honest with yourself?"

He finally lifted his head up and said," It was hot that day. Some people offered me some bear and I took it. I didn't think that I did anything wrong. Can I still be in the color guard?"

I just looked at him and said," I really am proud of you for your honesty. I know how much you enjoy marching with this color guard. It took a lot of courage to say that. I admire you for that. Unfortunately, I cannot let you come back into the group after you broke the rules. I can suggest that you join another drum corps color guard. You have a lot of potential and I hate to see it wasted. But now you have to do something that is going to be very hard for you. You have to go out there and tell your mother the truth."

He just looked at me and asked," You can't do that for me?"

I looked at him and said," No, this is something I think you need to do on your own."

I then tapped him on his left shoulder and said," You have been a good man for us. I have enjoyed teaching you. And you have grown a lot since joining the color guard."

He then went out to speak to his mother. After about ten minutes of very emotional conversations they left.

Needless to say this incident had a major impact on our performance that year. We ended up losing the Connecticut State Championship, winning the Massachusetts State Championship, retaining the Robert Grover Memorial trophy, and we also won the Northeastern States Championship. And every competition in between we lost that year.

We had a major impact to our color guard and that was almost impossible to over come.

One good thing did come out of it. The young man, whom I had released from the color guard, did join another organization. And he was their premiere person in that organization. In fact he ended up competing against Scott for the Individual rifle that year. Scott won. I was still proud of the job the other young man did.

All during that year Mark, his brother John, and Scott would often come over the house to visit. We were becoming close friends. I was teaching them chess. And Mark was learning all of the hidden meanings of that game. His insights were really surprising me. They were growing. And I knew it. They were growing into individuals that I was proud to know. Mark had even gotten a job as a manager of a convenience store in the center of town to earn some extra money. He really impressed me in the way he was growing up. And as the next season came close to starting I felt good about it and the competing color guar that year.

Then, on the morning of the following Memorial Day, I received a strange phone call from Mark's father. He was crying while he was speaking. He said: " Mark is dead."

I was in such a state of shock I could only respond with: " What? What happened?"

All of the emotions of what happened to Bobby, and Danny, came rushing back to me all over again.

Then Mark's father explained that the police had just left there. They had told him that the convenience store that Mark managed was robbed. The thief had put Mark in the Walk-in cooler and shot him in the back of the head. He also asked if I could take care of the Drum Corps that day.

I was stunned. I could only say: " Sure."

That whole day was a blur for me. All I could think of was the loss of another close friend. Another young man with unlimited potential had died. It is extremely harder to deal with this time. The funeral was another drum corps funeral. The feelings of loss came back to me and I was having a hard time with all of the emotions. All I could remember was the two infants, and Bobby and Danny. The tears were flowing heavily. Mark's father just couldn't stop crying that day. For he had just needlessly lost his first-born child and his pain was unbearable. The color guard all cried at losing a good friend and leader. They also dedicated there upcoming season to him.

All this was very familiar to me. Too familiar to me. And yet I understood how they felt and do you know what? They did it. They won everything that year. In fact that year it was all done **for Mark**.

The next season started with the usual Memorial Day parade. We were once again marching in three parades that day. This was the first parade in Westfield. Just before the parade started Mark's father started experiencing chest pains. He had to sit down under a tree because of the severity of the pain. We got the medics over to him as quickly as we could.

The pains were so severe that the medics there called for the ambulance. Before the ambulance came Mark's father called me over and said, " Mike can you take care of the corps today."

Eddie, my old color guard instructor was there at the time. He had come to wish me luck at the start of another drum Corps season. He just looked at me and said, " You take care of the Drum Corps. We will take care of him."

The corps marched off in that parade leaving him behind waiting for the ambulance. We were all in a state of panic. We were leaving our Corps director behind and it didn't feel good at all. And yet we knew that he would want us to do a good job that day. And that was the only reason why we tried.

When we, the drum corps, were about a mile down the road the ambulance, with its siren screaming came by us. The only thing I could say, to myself, was," I sure hope that he is going to be all right. He and his family have suffered enough with losing Mark."

The only thing I could think of was that it was a year earlier that Mark had died and his father did not look like he was going to make it. The parade felt like it took forever. I couldn't wait for it to be over. I just wanted to know that Mark's father, my friend, was going to be all right.

When we got to the end of the parade that day Eddie was there. He had a very serious look about him. He pulled me aside and told me that Mark's father had died on the way to the hospital. I was in complete shock. I slumped up against a tree for support. I didn't know how to react. I was in complete shock. When the rest of the corps found out they just had one question: " What should we do?"

I didn't understand where it came from, but I found myself saying: " We will go on to the next parade. And at the end of the day we will mourn the loss of our good friend."

It had taken all of the strength I had to muster up that response and once again I felt drained. That was a hard day for the drum corps. But they did what I had asked.

Now I was standing at the start of another Memorial Day parade with all of these memories coming back to me after Doug had asked that question. Namely, how I was doing?

It was at that moment that I realized two things.

The first was that I could no longer continue instructing the color guard. The emotional pain of losing so many good friends was reoccurring now, and I wasn't

dealing well with it. I had often wondered why Eddie and Gary had both left instructing. And now I understood. The emotional side was overpowering and starting to swell over to my daily life. No matter what I did I couldn't get it out of my thoughts.

Deep in my mind I realized that I knew this day was coming during the winter practice season. The color guard that was going out for competition that year was not ready. And it was all because I could no longer do it. I had lied to myself. I had told myself that they would do what the others before them had done. That is that they would learn as they went along through the season. All during the practice time during that year I new that they were not ready. And it was because of me. I just didn't have it in me anymore.

And yet how could I leave something that I had loved so much? How could I leave something that had defined me as the man I had become? Through all these questions I knew I had to leave. Emotionally I could not deal with the pain anymore. Now all I could do was look around at the color guard and wonder how many of them would end up dying before their time.

The second thing that I knew was that there were a lot of emotions in me that

I had to deal with. From the time of the twin babies dying I had tried to hold my emotions in. and in some respects, I was successful.

The emotions of the loss of close friends, such as Bobby, Danny, Mark, and his father were all coming back to me now. And then on top of all that a surprising thought came to me.

During the Viet Nam war two of my closes boyhood friends had died. And the only thing I could think of was the number of friends I had lost that I had never cried for. This thought bothered me a lot.

The parade was getting ready to start now. The color guard Sergeant called them together to get them ready. The Drum corps started up with a familiar song. The crowds were starting to gather at the entrance point of the parade. Then as the color guard was ready to step off I went over to where they were with tears in swelling in my eyes. I walked over to the right side of the line and said, "Let's walk."

As we stepped off for the parade I could feel my body slumping. It was being weighted down by the emotions that were running through my mind. I was struggling to put one foot in front of the other. Every step felt like it took a great deal of effort to perform.

All I could think of was the number of my close friends that had died by violent means. It weighted me down even more.

Then I heard a roar from the crowd.

Out of response I looked up to see what had caused it. And it was our drum corps that they were responding to. I was impressed.

I looked over to see how the color guard was doing. And they were doing great. They were good. Almost as good as the one I had marched in, and I knew it. I felt a glimmer of pride starting to swell inside me. This led me to remember a few things. Things that I had forgotten about.

I remembered what it was like seeing the color guard for the first time. And how their precision had completely amazed me.

I remembered how proud I was the day that Eddie handed out our uniforms to us.

I remembered how great it felt to complete our first parade. Especially since we completed *three parades in one day.*

I remembered how proud I was when we won our first competition.

And the memory of the first Northeastern Championship title came back to me with extreme pride.

With each of these memories I felt that glimmer of pride begin to swell inside me. It was getting larger and larger. I still felt slumped over but my feet were reacting to this feeling of pride and I knew it.

Then there was something else I remembered that made me chuckle inside. It had turned out that one of the parents of a member of the color guard was so impressed by how his son had changed through marching with us that he wanted to do something for me because of it. Whenever he saw me he would ask the same question," What can I do for you to pay you back for how you have helped my son?"

I could never come up with an answer. He just kept asking the same question whenever he saw me. Finally I gave in, and came up with an answer as a lark. I just wanted to stop him from asking that question. It turns out that he was a contractor by trade. So as a lark I told him, " Name a street after me."

He didn't say a word after that. And then about two months later I got a phone call from him. He asked me to do him a favor. I said," Sure. What is it?"

He then asked me to go to a certain location and let him know what I find there. So I did. And would you believe it, I found was a street named after me. I called him and thanked him. I even tried to explain that I wasn't serious about that request. He just didn't want hear about it. To me it was just a lark. Away of getting him to stop asking that question. To him it was something else. It turns out that he had spoken to a couple of friends of his about this incident. The reason I knew was because they had called me to tell me that they had also named streets after me. I was embarrassed. Needless to say I was going to think about how I answered questions like that in the future.

I once again looked to see how the color guard was doing. And once again I started remembering things.

I remembered receiving a complementary copy of a unique book in the mail one day.

It was accompanied with a sheet explaining what the book was all about. The book was,

The Who's who of Drum Corps. And according to the explanation it was the definitive list of the countrywide drum corps leaders, and their accomplishments, for the previous year. I was impressed that someone had taken the time to put a book like that together. The accompanying memo went on to explain that an individual had to be nominated for entrance into this document by at least three people. And then they researched the validity of the nomination. I was again impressed.

For the fun of it I started leafing through the book. I found Eddie's name in it. And that impressed me. Then I found Bill's name, our Drum Major, and that was also impressive to me. And then I found my name. What a shock. To be listed with these two giants of drum corps really surprised me.

And then I remembered being nominated for the Drum Corps Hall of fame. And this one I also chuckled at to myself. It was a great honor. Don't get me wrong; I was impressed that someone would nominate me for such an honor. According to the paperwork I had received on the subject I was nominated as a marcher as well as an instructor. The only thing they requested was for me to fill out my bibliography, and then they, the members of the acceptance team, would vote on my acceptance. Well that definitely gave me a way out. I never filled out the bibliography. I told everyone it was because I didn't instruct this color guard to be winning honors. That was enough to satisfy anyone who had asked me about it. The truth was I was embarrassed. After all I was just doing what I was taught by Eddie and the Grover Brothers. And if that was enough to be nominated for that honor they were really the ones that should be nominated and not I.

When I looked at the color guard they were receiving loud cheers throughout this segment of the parade. I was proud of the job they were doing.

I can feel the pride swelling even more inside me now, as I remembered something even more important to me. It was the feeling of pride I had while marching with the four Grover brothers. They were the best at what we did. And just being around them was a great learning experience for me. And to me I was proud of every moment I spent with them.

And it wasn't just me that they had impressed. Ever since they marched in this color guard they have inspired hundreds of people with their accomplishments. I was proud of the fact that all of these people wanted to emulate them. They had set a standard that hundreds of people had strived to accomplish.

To me we had accomplished something *great* during our time together. Something that very few people would ever experience. I knew that someone in the future would accomplish it again some day. But for our time it was still something *great*.

I could feel more pride swelling in me now. I was beginning to walk a little taller now. I could feel the physical change starting to take place.

I looked over to the color guard. They were still doing well. It showed me that they had learned. And that thought started me thinking about what I had learned through the years.

It was Eddie who had taught me how to teach a color guard and to become a better person. It was Bill who had taught me about the realities of life. And it was Jack, our first drum corps director, who had taught me that we can all do much more if we try. And my mother had taught me that I could accomplish whatever I put my mind to.

Of all of the things I had learned one stuck out the most to me. And surprisingly enough it came from the combination of, Bobby, Danny, Mark, and his father. It was that you have to love life. It is too short to ignore it. They had all loved life and that was important to them. Yes, I was finally admitting that I had learned something from the loss of these people. And that made the message even more important to me.

We were coming to the end of the parade now. I was walking more erect now with a renewed pride. I knew that I was leaving the drum corps. But I also knew that it was time for me to do so. I had learned everything I could during this journey and it was time for me to go and learn something else. And if I could share with someone what I had learned along the way it would be even better.

As we got to the end of the parade I was completely comfortable with my decision. I had learned a lot during my experiences with this organization and it was time for me to continue my growth.

The parade was over now. The Sergeant, of the color guard, was giving the members of the color guard instructions on how they should take care of their equipment before we went on to our next parade that day.

And right then and there I realized something. I wasn't the only one that had learned something through this experience.

They had also learned. And then I realized that they had learned everything that they needed to know. For it was completely true that they also had learned what it was like to practice something *until you could not get it wrong.*

CPSIA information can be obtained at www.ICGtesting.com
Printed in the USA
BVOW08*2336120116

432635BV00002B/12/P